A Short History of Copyright

Benedict Atkinson • Brian Fitzgerald

A Short History of Copyright

The Genie of Information

Springer

Benedict Atkinson
Faculty of Law
Australian Catholic University
Sydney, New South Wales
Australia

Brian Fitzgerald
Faculty of Law
Australian Catholic University
Melbourne, Victoria
Australia

The Work is based on the Introductions to the previously published Work: The Library of Essays on Copyright Law by Ashgate Publishing Limited, 2011, ISBN 978-0754628460. Published by kind permission of Ashgate Publishing Limited

ISBN 978-3-319-37707-0 ISBN 978-3-319-02075-4 (eBook)
DOI 10.1007/978-3-319-02075-4
Springer Cham Heidelberg New York Dordrecht London

Printed on acid-free paper

Springer is part of Springer Science+Business Media (www.springer.com)

Contents

Chapter 1
Introduction

Copyright history matters because, so far as copyright regulation is concerned, the past informs the present. Copyright policy—the reasons given for laws—is highly contested, in a way that most legal policy is not. Lawyers, for example, argue about interpretation or application of contract law principles. Few argue about the principles, because they are agreed. By contrast, consensus about copyright policy does not exist, unless the consensus is the consensus of a faction. Should production and supply of information be controlled? How should it be controlled? Who controls? How? What is the social effect of control? The economic effect? Does control have a future? What might that future be? The copyright hegemon, a global network of rules and interests governing supply and consumption of information, shapes economic activities and our interpretation of the world. Some say that the hegemon must expire, unable to reconcile internal contradictions. Others argue that reduction of proprietary rights invites chaos. No one knows the future. This book tries to explain the past to help us understand the present and think constructively about what may lie ahead.

B. Atkinson and B. Fitzgerald, *A Short History of Copyright*,
DOI 10.1007/978-3-319-02075-4_1,

Chapter 2
Origins

2.1 What Is Copyright?

Copyright is a form of property created by statute.[1] The first national copyright codes were passed in the United Kingdom in 1710 and in the United States in 1790 but the origins of copyright law can be traced from the social, political and legal thought of Greece and Rome, and the history of property relations in western Europe.[2] In other parts of the world, different societies developed conceptions of ownership similar to those of European societies. Some defined title in very different ways, and others bypassed any notion of possessive individual ownership.[3]

Copyright confers on the authors of works and the companies that make products embodying works—or control the means of disseminating works—exclusive rights. These are economic rights. They enable authors and producers to control the process of producing and disseminating copyright material for sale (although the copyright owner also controls most non-economic uses of material).

---

[1] Sir William Blackstone, in his *Commentaries on the Laws of England* (1766) famously called property the 'sole despotic dominion which one man claims and exercises over the external things of the world, in total exclusion of the right of any other individual in the universe'. A shorter way of expressing Blackstone's proposition is to say that property is that which the law makes subject to a person's exclusive control. Property is anything (including things abstract) that is definable, and defined, and which legislators agree may be controlled, or owned, by people (or a proxy, like a company).

[2] In France, monarchs granted limited printing patents from the sixteenth century. In the throes of revolution, a decree of 1793 created authors' rights in France (*Décret de la Convention Nationale du dix-neuf juillet 1793 relatif aux droits de propriété des Auteurs d'écrits en tout genre, des Compositeurs de musique, des Peintres et des Dessinateurs (avec le rapport de Lakanal)* or Decree of the National Convention, of 19 July 1793, concerning authors' property rights in all types of writing and the rights in their work of composers of music, painters and illustrators). Codification in civil law countries followed in the nineteenth century creating copyrights that recognized *droit d'auteur* including moral rights.

[3] See discussion of obligation-based society.

B. Atkinson and B. Fitzgerald, *A Short History of Copyright*,
DOI 10.1007/978-3-319-02075-4_2,

Although the exclusive rights are primarily economic in function, the author to whom the rights accrue also enjoys moral rights, which are personal rights. Personal rights, unlike the exclusive rights, are normally not assignable. They benefit the author alone and are usually extinguished when the author dies or when copyright lapses.[4]

In the English-speaking world, moral rights usually consist of the rights of attribution (to be named the author of the work) and integrity (to prevent adaptations or uses of the work that depart from the integrity of the work as conceived by the author). In civil law countries, in which economic rights are understood to derive from moral rights, moral rights are more extensive in scope.[5]

Moral rights of any complexion can be traced to the French-inspired civil law conception of copyright as regulation that recognizes the innate value of the author's vocation. French custom characterizes copyright as an author's right or *droit d'auteur*, a term that recognizes that in addition to moral rights (*le droit moral*), the author possesses entitlement to economic reward (*le droit patrimonial*).[6]

An account of copyright that refers to exclusive rights and moral rights is, however, incomplete. More than most other categories of law, copyright law was, and is, shaped by social and economic forces with deep historical roots. Copyright works consist of *information*, the lifeblood of cultural development, exchange and evolution. All societies, dependent on communication for survival, intrinsically are interested in the supply of information. Information is a source of enlightenment and freedom. The way society regulates information supply expresses how society thinks about people and how they are entitled to live.

2.2 Possession and Exclusion

The Stoic philosophers of Greece and later Rome postulated the idea that various formulas for devising proprietary rights are attempts to express the natural law. The correct formula merely expressed principles immanent in the natural world. Thus the Roman categories of property based on the concept of absolute possession found justification in nature. From the time when Roman law first articulated the

---

[4] The Berne Convention for the Protection of Literary and Artistic Works (1886) provides that moral rights survive the death of the author and are exercisable, at least until copyright is extinguished, by persons or institutions nominated in legislation (Article 6 *bis*). The legislation of some countries, such as France, provides for moral rights to exist in perpetuity.

[5] In France, moral rights consist of, in addition to the rights of attribution and integrity, the rights of publication and withdrawal (see *Code de la propriété intellectuelle* or Intellectual Property Code).

[6] The French law, however, is called the *Code de la propriété intellectuelle*. French legal usage has increasingly accepted the Anglo-Saxon term 'intellectual property' to signify that copyright protection applies to 'intellectual' output. Increasingly, lawyers use the term *droit intellectuelle* to describe copyright.

owner's *dominium* and, later, when the jurist emperor Justinian distinguished between tangible and abstract property,[7] the ideology of natural law supplied justifying theory for jurists explaining the owner's control.

Roman law bequeathed to the modern systems of common and civil law principles of property, the chief of which is the idea that possession confers ownership. The concept of ownership, expressed in the Latin word *dominium*, has recurred as the motif of social and political action in the Western world since the end of the Roman Empire in the fifth century. Ownership is the determinant of power. Insistence upon the right of authors, and later industries, to own whatever they produced created and expanded the modern law of copyright.

Because proprietary rights confer power, they are contested, and the events leading to the vesting of rights invariably occurred in the context of charged politics. Debates, however, were rarely resolved by simple political calculation. They usually involved intense dispute over assumptions and philosophies that were aired in ancient Greece, and then, over nearly 2,000 years, in the Roman world, and, later, in the societies of western Europe.

Disputes concerned the moral or economic necessity for granting ownership over land, things and definable abstractions. The main propositions debated have not varied greatly over the centuries. For example, faced with the prevailing belief that proprietary rights are justified in themselves, the early Fathers of the Catholic Church argued, especially in the third to fifth centuries, that the fruits of the earth are to be shared, not appropriated for private use. Though inspired by a unique teleology, their attitude resembled in part that of folklore-based indigenous society, and prefigured the communist conception of society without property.[8]

---

[7] Issued under the Emperor Justinian's direction, from AD 529–533, the *Corpus Juris Civilis*, consisting of the *Code*, *Novels*, *Institutes* and *Digest*, restated and expanded Roman law. The law explained abstract or incorporeal property by reference to incorporeal things and usufruct (see Book II Chapters II and IV of the Institutes). Justice Arthur Emmett of the Australian Federal Court has pointed out (conference paper 2011) that while Roman law did not recognise the right to control copying of works, it established principles that could later be adapted to define the categories of literary property and other species of copyright. In particular, the idea of usufruct, which referred to the right of a person to enjoy the fruits—the product, like farm produce, of something regenerative—of another's property, accommodates the idea of the author enjoying the fruit (royalties) of something regenerative (a literary work). The usufruct itself was an incorporeal thing, a legal interest. According to Emmett, if analogy is made between the Roman law of usufruct and modern law of copyright, the author has rights of usufruct which expire on death. Subject to usufruct, the work or property is in the public domain. However, Roman law did not recognise literary property.

[8] The Church Fathers, theologians and teachers from the eastern and western empire, spoke vehemently, in sermons and writings over a number of centuries, against the accumulation of possessions and the exclusion of the poor from the benefits of those possessions. A number, especially St Iranaeus (130–202), St Basil the Great (329–79), St Ambrose (340–97), St Augustine (354–430) and St John Chrysostom (347–407) attacked covetousness and selfishness—the 'pride of life' (1 John 2:16)—that led some to concentrate wealth while neglecting to share for the common good.

Centuries before the Fathers, the Greek philosopher Plato (427–347 BC) in the *Republic* and *Laws* proposed a society in which community of interest made private property a redundant concept. His pupil Aristotle (384–322 BC), though he shared Plato's view that concentration of ownership is socially harmful,[9] considered private property a consequence of human existence, reflecting an innate desire for private possession. Aristotelian ethics concentrated little on the existence of property and much more on the way in which citizens exercised proprietary rights. Aristotle's idea of property as a social good if available to all, and exercised in ways consistent with public benefit, strongly influenced the social teaching of the Catholic Church.[10]

In the nineteenth century, the anarchist Pierre Proudhon, enraged that the great mill of capital maintained the owners in luxury and kept the workers in bondage, their lives eked out in tenements, reached conclusions similar to those of the Church Fathers over 1,500 years earlier. He looked at the city proletariat and asked the question 'What is property?' His famous reply has ever since resonated in debate over property rights: '*It is robbery!*'[11]

The theme of exclusion runs through the history of property relations. Its antithesis is the modern idea of a copyright 'commons', a source of communal exchange from which no one is excluded. Ideas of copyright and commons have co-existed uneasily for over a century, and today in political debate over copyright the commons is seen to infringe on private rights. For their part, supporters of the commons regard statutory copyright as a moveable feast, encroaching, to the point of complete possession, on the notional terrain of free inquiry and exchange.

While arguments over the scope of copyright may appear bloodless, their implications are not negligible. It is by consulting the history leading up to the creation of statutory copyright that we understand the extent to which the law of copyright represents political and philosophical assumptions that remain contested.

2.3 Social Change Determines Rules About Information

To understand the law of copyright, it is important to look at how philosophies and social movements influenced its development. This is both an historical and a comparative exercise. A history of copyright law development necessarily focuses on the story of legislative changes in the United Kingdom and United States, and various civil law countries, chiefly France.

---

[9] In the *Republic*, Plato posited, in the dialogues of Socrates, that private property—and money—encouraged in humans hatred, plotting and fear. He advocated, initially, a *polis* governed by 'guardians' who live without property or family.

[10] Aristotle, *Politics*, Book II, Pt V.

[11] Proudhon (1840/1994).

The history of information regulation is also a history of social development. For most of human history in most of the world, a hierarchy of authority—tribal elders, emperors, kings, magistrates, judges, bishops and so on—controlled the dissemination of information to the general population. The emergence of copyright law represents a shift in societal norms, from acceptance of authority and hierarchy, towards assertion of individual or private interests, and the demand for ownership of things produced.

Approaches to the regulation of information historically fell into two classes: obligation-based and entitlement-based. In obligation-based society, each class in the social hierarchy carried out its duties and respected the trust—or obligations—bestowed on it. Social quiesence characterized such societies since individuals accepted their unchanging status, and fixed function, within the society.

Entitlement-based society repudiates the idea of a fixed social order and substitutes, in place of social obligation, the individual freedom, in a contested environment, to accrue material benefit. By labour the individual becomes entitled to those benefits, in other words to own property, and ownership confers sovereignty. Acting within the law, the owner is free to use property as he or she chooses, and to exclude any other person from its benefits.

2.4 Obligation-Based Society and Attitudes to Information

In most societies, for most of history, the obligation to obey has channelled the creative impulse into communal rather than individual expression. For this reason, perhaps, such societies have not been preoccupied with attributing individual works to individual authors.[12] Literacy did not necessarily, or even usually, result in ideas of authorial entitlement.

Indigenous peoples, often nomadic, have, sometimes over thousands of years, observed ancient cultural norms that reflect knowledge of the complex elements of their physical environment. They have expressed symbolically and metaphorically, in stories and legend, the meaning of existence and the purpose of society. But their expressive tradition is not intended to communicate to a foreign audience, the knowledge contained in it is sometimes secret, and each adult member of the group is charged with the obligation to honour the social or communal purpose of tribal or group culture.

Obligation of this sort is unlikely to precipitate individual appropriation of knowledge for private gain. In short, the social norms of indigenous people are

[12] An animist tribe obeying the edicts of elders fulfilled obligations to honour ancestors by living in certain ways in the physical environment. Before European penetration, many non-European societies, including the indigenous cultures of North America and Australia, shared knowledge about their natural surroundings, including the medicinal properties of plants, and collected and retold folklore and other stories. But they had no conception of individual entitlement: tales about nature, stories about people, were a collective inheritance.

often incompatible with the possessive, self-maximizing coda of proprietary rights that has pertained in the Western world for many centuries. Indigenous peoples living in traditional society are thus vulnerable to proprietary appropriation, by predatory commercial interests, of ancient knowledge, and the expressions of their tradition, such as artwork.[13]

In China, over millennia, neither literacy among the educated nor the invention of printing[14] led to a strong tradition of authors' rights or property in literary works. Confucianism instilled primary allegiance to the emperor, who represented the state, and secondary allegiance to the patriarchal family. The state discouraged self-expression (except through controlled channels) and declared itself owner of the works of artists. After invention of printing during the Tang Dynasty (618–908 AD) the imperial government represented itself as a protector, supposedly controlling printing to prevent alien ideas from corrupting the population.[15]

Neither absence of regulation resembling copyright, nor the burden of avoiding offence to the court, stymied growth, in parts of China, of a flourishing commercial book trade. Before the ninth century AD, printers published mainly Buddhist devotional works before expanding into genres including poetry and medical manuals. Then in Song, Ming and Qing periods (ending 1279, 1644 and 1911), diverse literature, much of it fiction, contributed (by late Ming) to 'an early mass communications society,' partly politicised by a shisang literati-merchant-business class. Like Europeans publishing tracts and pamphlets for more than two centuries after publication of Gutenberg's Bible (1452), the shisang may, in the same period, have used print, obliquely, to destabilise political authority. Only partly circumscribed by threat of repression, and unrestricted by legal prohibition of copying, Chinese publishing into the twentieth century created high and low literary cultures, usually in parallel to, and sometimes informing, political process.[16] In India, an extensive vedic literature in Sanskrit began to appear in the sixteenth century BC and for nearly a 1,000 years from around the sixth century BC, Indian writers recorded the precepts and stories of Hinduism in the *Mahabharata*.[17] The text, including the book's most famous part, the

---

[13] See, for instance, discussion of the relevance of traditional cultural obligations in the production of indigenous artworks in the Australian case of *John Bulun Bulun & Anor* v. *R & T Textiles Pty Ltd* [1998] Federal Court of Australia, 1082 (3 September 1998) at www.austlii.edu.au. See also discussion in the Australian publication, *Our Culture Our Future: Report on Australian Indigenous Cultural and Intellectual Property Rights* (Janke 1998).

[14] Woodblock printing for textiles appeared in China around AD 220 and ceramic movable type came into use in the eleventh century. A court official and a scholar invented wooden and metallic movable types in the fourteenth and fifteenth centuries respectively.

[15] See Alford (1995). See also Holcombe (1992).

[16] Meyer-Fong (2007).

[17] The author of the *Mahabharata*, including the *Bhagavad Gītā*, is said to be Vyasa, a mythic figure who appears in the text. Anonymous writers contributed, over many centuries, to the threefold enlargement of the original document. In the fourth century BC, the *Ramayana*, an epic poem written in Sanskrit, and attributed by Hindu tradition to the sage Valmiki, appeared in India and came to influence Indian culture co-extensively with the *Mahabharata*.

Bhagavad Gītā, continued over centuries to contribute to popular acceptance, in most of the subcontinent, of Hindu ontology.

Vyasa is declared by tradition author of the *Mahabharata*, but no one remembers his successors, the anonymous elaborators of the work. They were, so far as the teachers of Hinduism were concerned, scribes of the numinous, giving material form to the truth about existence. Authorship and dissemination helped to create Indian society, but works created were the possession of society not authors.[18]

Mughal rule in India, beginning in the early sixteenth century, and the liberal use of the printing press, introduced from Europe, produced a diffuse literature written in Urdu and other languages of the subcontinent. The Mughals encouraged poetry, translation of Sanskrit literature, works of history, even works of fiction. But in a linguistically diverse and sometimes politically fragmented country, ideas of property in literature were alien. The Mughal court remained the locus of literary patronage. Literature united society according to the pattern decided by the imperial centre, and the idea of possessive authorship, of literature belonging to its authors, remained largely unknown.

In societies that do not recognize possessive values, expressed in the language of 'I' and 'mine' and the restless desire for accumulation, dissemination is usually a favoured instrument for creating social cohesion. In a non-individualist, obligation-based society, culture is created to shape society not profit the creator. In such a society, however, the Western mode of cultural production may not automatically be regarded as alien, and authorial rights may be recognised.

Modern Islamic society draws on a rich and diverse literary and artistic heritage that began nearly fifteen centuries ago. While contemporary Muslim society in the Middle East increasingly affirms the value of legal protection of abstract property, the Muslim tradition, which clearly delineated proprietary rights in tangible things, did not categorically recognize property in intangibles. Literary and artistic production, over the centuries, tended to be commissioned by, or produced under the auspices of, royal or well-connected patrons.

The dynamic capitalism that stimulated the growth of book trades in the English-speaking world never pertained in the Middle East, so the motive of commercial gain, which played so large a role in Western agitations for proprietary rights, did not inspire in Muslim countries a commensurate demand for abstract property rights. But Islamic scholars have not declared that Islamic or Shariah law could apply only to tangible property.[19]

---

[18] The Mughal invasion of India resulted in the creation of a different tradition in which poets, historians and writers patronized by the court flourished (see e.g. Losty and Roy 2012).

[19] See Raslan (2007), pp. 497–559.

2.5 Recognition of Authors

The recognition of authors is identifiable (though not exclusively) with a cultural outlook that emerged first in ancient Greece, and spread through the Roman world. From the second century BC, until the breakdown of the empire, Romans appear to have accepted that authors were entitled to profit in some way from their work.[20]

Writers during the classical period of Latin, lasting 200–300 years from the late republican period, published to instruct, entertain or persuade a critical public, usually mindful of one censoring power or another. Plutarch, a Greek, tells the story of how a grandson of Caesar Augustus, afraid to show liking for the Republic's greatest literary defender, hid from his grandfather his copy of one of Cicero's works. Augustus took no offence. He told the boy that Cicero was 'a lover of his country.'[21]

How much authors received pecuniary benefit from the transmission of their works is not known. Augustus sponsored Virgil, the great classical poet, but it does not seem likely that the Roman literary system depended on patronage. Catullus, the extraordinary, shortlived, poet of feeling, who vanishes from historical record about 53 BC, came to Rome apparently endowed with some wealth from his equestrian family. Julius Caesar dictated works for political purposes, and supported himself from immense plunder. Only in the later imperial period, following work of Roman jurists in defining categories of property—and the legal status of quasi-possessions, such as the right to sue for a debt—does a clear basis for establishing literary property seem to emerge.[22]

The common law system first formally recognized literary property, the common name for copyright in books, in 1710, when the British parliament passed the Statute of Anne. However, the idea of a person's right to exclusively possess printed works long preceded this date. Although print monopolies existed in the fifteenth century, a convenient marker of the shift in European societies towards recognition of modern categories of private property, including literary property, is the Protestant Reformation.

Out of that religious rupture came societies that accepted, in some degree, an idea announced earlier by the Italian Renaissance: man, reaching for the heavens,

---

[20] The nineteenth-century author Walter Copinger, author of the famous English legal textbook *The Law of Copyright* (1870—now in its 15th edition as *Copinger and Skone James on Copyright*) argued that the Roman world embraced a notion of literary property. According to Copinger, the Roman playwright Terence (d. 159 BC) sold copies of *Eununchus* and *Hecyra*, and the poet Statius (AD 45–96) sold copies of *Agave*.

[21] Plutarch (1968). Cicero's opposition to Mark Antony, expressed in the *Philippics*, led to his proscription and murder by Mark Antony in 43 BC. Octavian, then allied to Antony, but later victor over him in civil war, consented to proscription of Cicero.

[22] The *Institutes* of Justinian (AD 533) distinguished between corporeal and incorporeal property and they also interpreted the doctrine of *accessio* or merger to favour, in some circumstances, ownership by the artist of objects embodying art. Whether the artist owned the object seemed to depend on the quality of the art (*Institutes* 2.1 33–34).

is free to shape his destiny. How European nations interpreted this idea differed, but after the Reformation, all moved away from the medieval conception of the artist as an anonymous contributor to public expressions of God's glory. In England especially, the author began gradually to step into public sight, and, more prominently, the bookseller, proto-publisher and proto-capitalist, who actually benefitted from print monopolies.

Underpinning the idea of literary property is the idea of entitlement. Output is not an obligation but the result of positive choice, and one deserving reward. In the case of printed output, said the booksellers of the sixteenth century, the reward of output, and the guarantee of its continuation, must be monopoly control of the process of production and distribution.

2.6 The Origins of Entitlement

Recognition of authors followed centuries of feudalism in Europe, during which a few writers might be acknowledged for a religious work or even works of general literature. But the notion of authorship, accepted in the Roman world, stagnated in feudal society, and devotional or academic treatises, and even a few diversionary works, were written for instruction or entertainment, not fame or fortune.

The feudal world of Europe came slowly into existence after the breakdown of Roman institutions in western Europe after the fifth century, and lasted for nearly a millennium. Only as feudalism broke down in the fifteenth century, did attitudes to information change. In preceding centuries, the accepted modes of social exchange precluded the dynamic exchange of information that later resulted in creation of the copyright system. Atrophy rather than dynamism characterized the process of spreading information.

In the feudal world, no one could have conceived of proprietary rights in information. Medieval notions of property relied on the concept of *trusteeship*. Man received all things from God, and *enjoyed* the use of these things in trust from God. Trust imposed obligations but the complex web of relationships that bound superiors and inferiors restricted the transmission of information. Fixed social relations caused curiosity to atrophy, forestalling inquiry and debate.

On the other hand, the feudal tenure system limited the extent to which Crown, church and nobility could insist on their absolute possession of landholdings. Lords made available to common people, for grazing and cultivation, their 'waste' lands which they could not, or chose not to, use for private purposes. These wastelands became known as the 'commons'.[23]

[23] On the history of common land, see Clark and Clark (2001), pp. 1009–1036. The authors estimate that by 1500 common land constituted only one-third of total land in England and by 1600, waste (land unencumbered by any proprietary restrictions) only 4 % of total land.

2.7 A New Conception of Property

A new idea of private property began to emerge in western Europe in the early medieval period, when jurists and teachers, or scholastics, discussed at universities the morality of ownership. The greatest scholastic is St Thomas Aquinas (d. 1274), and his dialectics concerning the legitimacy of possession presaged the later emergence of expanding, diversifying economies, in which elaboration of proprietary rights made possible widespread credit and commerce.

Already, in the time of Aquinas, an assertive political class, intent on material gain, and irked by spiritual restriction, rejected belief that on earth humans must be conforming creatures, and substituted a precept of illimitable self. Selfhood is the source of improvement, and achievement is the product of individual agency. Aquinas would not have assented to these ideas. However, by departing from aspects of patristic tradition, he helped, unwittingly, to precipitate movement towards intellectual acceptance of possessive attitudes.

The Fathers considered that natural law rejected property as alien to nature—though they allowed that its existence is inevitable, and therefore that mode of possession or use, not possession itself, determines whether a particular instance of ownership is sinful—and Aquinas agreed with this proposition.[24] Natural law, according to Aquinas, does not comprehend private property. However, he said, natural law does not *forbid* private property.

Like the Fathers, Aquinas said that property is the consequence of original sin. Humans create property because they are imperfect creatures, with imperfect understanding of the divine order, which does not admit possession or exclusion. But they do so by applying their God-given faculty of reason to the surrounding world, as they should. Human law, the *ius gentium* justifies property, while *lex naturalis*, the natural law, justifies absolutely the community of property, that is, the society of sharing prescribed by the Fathers (in contradistinction to the worldly community of ownership).[25]

Aquinas thus justified property, whereas the patristic teachers considered private possession, in principle, to result from moral failure.[26] Aquinas, like the Fathers, insisted that owners are obliged to obey the natural law. Unlike them, he

[24] Chroust and Affeldt (1950–1951).

[25] *Id.*

[26] 'The possession of all things in common is ascribed to the natural law; not in the sense that the natural law dictates that all things should be possessed in common, and that nothing should be possessed as one's own; but in the sense that no division of property is made by the natural law. This division arose from human agreement which belongs to the positive law .... Hence the ownership of possessions is not contrary to the natural law, but a super-addition thereto devised by human reason.' (St Thomas Aquinas *Summa Theologica* 2.2 quaest art 2 ad 1).

characterised property as 'super-added' to natural law, and thus created a theory of property that would be interpreted to admit departure from the Christian ethic of solidarity.[27]

Since property confers on the owner a right to exclude, in principle the existence of property undermines the patristic ideal of solidarity. Aquinas's endorsement of proprietary rights represents a beginning in the political movement towards endorsement of rights of ownership and property, including property in information.

References

Alford WP (1995) To steal a book is an elegant offense: intellectual property law in Chinese civilization. Stanford University Press, Stanford

Blackstone W (1766) Commentaries on the laws of England. Clarendon, Oxford

Chroust AH, Affeldt RJ (1950–1951) The problem of private property according to St Thomas Aquinas. Marquette Law Rev 34(3):151–182

Clark G, Clark A (2001) Common Rights to Land in England, 1475–1839. J Econ Hist 61(4):1009–1036

Emmett R (2011) Roman law, private property and the public domain: lessons for copyright policy. Queensland University of Technology E Prints 2011. Paper summarizing presentation at 'Blue Sky New Directions in Copyright', Conference, February 2011

Holcombe C (1992) The bonds of empire: liberty in early medieval China. The Historian 54(4):609–626

Janke T (1998) Our culture our future: report on Australian indigenous cultural and intellectual property rights. Prepared for the Australian Institute of Aboriginal and Torres Strait Islander Studies and the Aboriginal and Torres Strait Islander Commission. Michael Franke & Co Solicitors, Surry Hills

Losty JP, Roy M (2012) Mughal India: art culture and empire. British Library Publishing Division, London

Meyer-Fong T (2007) The printed world: books, publishing culture, and society in late imperial China. J Asian Stud 66(3):787–817

Plutarch (1968) Fall of the Roman Republic. Penguin, Harmondsworth

Proudhon PJ (1840/1994) What is property? An inquiry into the principle of right and of government (ed. and trans: Kelley DR, Smith BG). Cambridge University Press, Cambridge

Raslan HA (2007) 'Shari'a and the protection of intellectual property – the example of Egypt. IDEA Intellect Prop Law Rev 47:497–559

[27] The idea of 'solidarity' is central to patristic commentary, and the teaching of Catholic and Orthodox churches to the present. It encapsulates the Christian concept of equality, which is based on the principle that every person is, from conception, and without limitation, a child of God, called by God to express the volition implied in this identity: to find union with God by love (the essence of divine nature), to know God (to understand the meaning of love), and to serve God (a chief expression of love).

Chapter 3
Printing, Reformation and Information Control

3.1 Change

From the fourteenth to sixteenth centuries, overlapping phenomena—humanism, the Italian Renaissance, the Black Death, the invention of the moveable-type printing press and the Protestant Reformation—began to upend the obligation-based system of property relations. When the plague swept through Europe in the middle of the fourteenth century, killing one-third of the population, it rattled every institution of the medieval world, setting many peasants free from feudal obligations. Traumatized survivors saw that high birth, social status or spiritual rank did not protect a person from the undiscriminating hand of death.

Nearly a century after the outbreak of the Black Death (1348–50), came an event that more than any other pointed to the end of medievalism and the start of the new age that would eventually usher in the law and economy of copyright. In 1439, Johannes Gutenberg, a German goldsmith, perfected a mechanical printing press that reproduced copy using moveable type.

In the 1450s, he printed copies of the Bible, the so-called Gutenberg Bible. Imitations of Gutenberg's printing press spread swiftly through Europe and by the end of the century, publishers throughout Europe printed prolifically. The literate of any class could read or publish, in their own language, pamphlets, and even books.

Ideas and controversies inflamed minds across Europe, and a publishing frenzy ensued. Pamphlets followed books and more books. Foment eventually produced an earthquake, the Protestant Reformation. As humanism had spread across Europe, restless spirits in the north showed themselves less friendly to church precepts than the Italian progenitors of the new learning. Eventually, they created a popular intellectual revolt against Catholicism by remarkable use of the printing press.

B. Atkinson and B. Fitzgerald, *A Short History of Copyright*,
DOI 10.1007/978-3-319-02075-4_3, © Springer International Publishing Switzerland 2014

3.2 Protestant Reformation

For over a century until 1517, when Martin Luther nailed his 95 theses on the door of All Saints' Church at Wittenberg, dissenters such as the English Lollards and the Hussites in Bohemia, criticized, without much popular support, some ecclesiastical practices such as the issuing of indulgences. But Luther expressed his protest in print and his polemics were distributed in Europe, and especially Germany, in thousands, then hundreds of thousands, of pamphlets. When he drew to his cause disaffected German princes, he threw Europe into uproar.

In the disputatious atmosphere of the north, the intellectual openness of the southern Renaissance transformed into the fierce didacticism that became the hallmark of Luther and his followers. Luther's raging nature, and his willingness to fight spiritual warfare against an institution in existence for nearly one and a half millennia, suited very well the programme of the German princes and the money-making classes of the north. It freed them from the constraint of spiritual authority and allowed them to assert their wills in politics and commerce.

A 100 years of tumult followed Luther's death, and came to an end in the 1648 Peace of Westphalia. In the continuing struggles within societies, and between nations, the legacy of Gutenberg and Luther is unmistakable. The proselytizing use of the printing press may have transformed Europe but it is the genie of information that everywhere incited change and invited government suppression. The genie never returned to its bottle. It continues to shape society, to alarm authorities, to delight the curious. In the explosion of information from the sixteenth century until the present, the story of copyright finally takes shape.

3.3 Licensing

Political powers in most European countries responded to the spread of printing presses by trying to control supply of literature. They did so by granting printers the exclusive right to print pamphlets or books. Systematic licensing of printing, or the output of printing, was a novelty in Europe. In Greece, as in Rome, authorities usually reacted to the authors of objectionable views by disposing of offending writers. In China, emperors controlled publication of texts long before the practice of licensing began in Europe.

Licensing is indistinguishable from censorship insofar as the state, or equivalent authority, exercises power to prohibit printing and publication. Printers granted exclusive rights to print books, or permit printing, well knew, either from the terms of grant of privilege, or direct instruction from authorities, what literature could not be printed. From an early period, they performed the tasks of censors.

Though attitudes to censorship differed, the reason for prohibition did not. By licensing, authorities suppressed dissent, and, or so they believed, secured their survival. Power of prohibition links, in principle, licensing rights and copyright.

The copyright owner is not a censor, but copyright confers a right to prohibit others from copying the copyright holder's work.

Licensing usually operated by official grant to a printer, or printers, of the privilege of printing all literature permitted to be distributed in the domain. In 1486, republican Venice granted the first licence, or privilege, for publication of a history of Venice. Six years later, Venice issued new privileges for publication of books and continued to do so thereafter. By the end of the fifteenth century, European authors emerged in numbers. In 1506, the famous Dutch humanist Erasmus went to Italy, chiefly to find a publisher. He wanted to persuade the Venetian printer Aldus Manutius, 'a pioneer of finely printed popular editions' to publish his works.[1]

On the cusp of the Reformation, other states began to license production of literature. In 1501, the Holy Roman Empire's judicial council issued a licence to publish a drama. A papal bull prohibited unlicensed printing, and thereafter Popes granted printing privileges. The French Crown granted Parisian printers privileges in 1507. In 1512, the Holy Roman Empire issued the first general licence for publication of works.

In 1518, in England, the Crown established the office of King's Printer. All of these developments, occurring in something of a flurry, anticipated the coming religious whirlwind. That left in its wake sectarian politics of a character hitherto unseen in Europe, and politics of disputation, dissension and violence. Attachment to control of opinion by licensing grew, and in a later period, copyright legislation, granting authorial control, came into existence.

3.4 The Printing Industry in England

When Luther's revolution came to England in the years after 1517, its ideas received a cool official welcome for a number of years, until King Henry VIII's desire for a new wife resulted in estrangement between monarch and Pope, then excommunication, and the English Crown's rejection of papal authority. From these events sprang consequences that resulted in the licensing of books and ultimately the creation of statutory copyright.

The consequences included political changes that upturned English society, paving the way for the emergence, over 150 years, of an economically dynamic society receptive to the idea of literary property. In the same period, religious hostility encouraged political authorities to censor literature and proscribe books. In England the printers, who on the European continent spread religious and social protest, collaborated in, then oversaw, the process of censorship.

Why they did so is easy to explain. Though they may have varied in their views about the content of censored material, the principal London printers, members of

[1] Clark (1972) at p. 145.

the Stationers' Company, a London guild of bookbinders, printers and booksellers,[2] agreed that to prosper they must secure monopoly over printing in the kingdom. By seeking exclusive control of printing, they were at once true to the exclusionary ethos of their 200-year-old guild, and strikingly modern in their desire to control the market, crush competition and dominate supply. They were no less than precursors of the modern copyright industries, which rely on statutory monopolies to optimize revenue.

Printing came to England in 1477, when William Caxton published the first book printed in the country. Suddenly, capital became a crucial element in book production, and as the market increased, so did the fortunes of booksellers with the foresight and pockets to spot and supply demand. Inspired by European precedents, they tried to overcome competition by securing state-sanctioned monopoly. By the time of Henry VIII's excommunication in 1533, Crown grants, or letters patent, which gave booksellers the exclusive right to print a book, were not uncommon.

3.5 Political Revolution and Privatization

The invention of the printing press, and the grant of printing monopolies in Italy and France in the fifteenth century are the precursors of statutory copyright, but the politics of Tudor England provided the catalyst for the creation of an incipient form of copyright, and its successor, statutory copyright.

In Henry VIII's reign, the English political and merchant classes, including the printers and booksellers, cast off the last fetters of the old medieval economy, and embraced selfhood and material gain as primary motives for action. But they could only do so because to attain personal ends, Henry embarked upon political revolution, and in the course of that revolution, initiated an extraordinary programme of what is now called privatization—the creation of private property from public resources, or institutional property. In the case of Henry's privatization, the institution affected was the Catholic Church, and the property appropriated was that belonging to the monasteries.

Dissolution of the monasteries delivered a large portion of England into private hands but the process of privatization did not end with Henry's death. The act of privatization, involving appropriation and possession, the elements of ownership, became the accepted mode of creating industry and wealth. Property ownership became the emblem of social success. Once unleashed, the spirit of privatization continued to influence political action, complementing the growth of capitalism

[2] The Stationers were members of a guild consisting of allied trades recognized by the City of London in 1403. Their name recognized the dominant role of the booksellers, who contracted the services of other trades in the production of a book. Booksellers, the forerunners of modern publishers, played an integral part in the political and legal dramas that established the boundaries of statutory copyright in the eighteenth century.

until the present day. The law of copyright is merely one part of the story of privatization begun by Henry VIII.

That law, as we know it, can trace direct descent to the printing monopoly established after Henry's death by the Stationers' Company, a collective galvanized by the opportunities for economic preferment that seemed to proliferate in Henry's tumultuous reign. His programme created the conditions for the Stationers to seek control over the printing trade, and their eventual success in this enterprise resulted in a licensing system only definitively extinguished by the creation of the first copyright statute in 1710.

3.6 Attack on the Monasteries

Henry set sail on the course of revolution in 1532 when, with the assistance of Cranmer, the Archbishop of Canterbury, a covert Protestant, he divorced his wife, Catherine of Aragon, and married Anne Boleyn. He thus found himself in a double-bind. In danger of excommunication by the Pope, who upheld the sacramental validity of his marriage to Catherine, and beholden to Cranmer's theology, which justified his actions, Henry faced a Rubicon: accept the Pope's authority and his own error, or press forward in rebellion.

For Henry, there was no turning back and the Pope excommunicated him in 1533. Though Henry considered himself faithful to his baptism, and disliked the anti-sacramental reform programme of the Protestants, he also insisted on the supremacy of his will. So he set out to create a national church of catholic character but subordinate to the Crown's authority, and inevitably ran into the problem of persuading much of the clergy, and the population outside London, of the validity of reform.

Henry's bellicose nature determined his response to opposition. He sought to reduce or destroy rather than conciliate. Thus when the Crown's financial crisis became pressing,[3] he launched the most radical phase of the political revolution that began with the break from Rome, embarking upon land seizure on an enormous scale. The monasteries and other branches of the English Catholic Church held land occupying about a quarter of England. His coffers emptied, Henry hungered for this rich patrimony.

In 1536, urged on by Protestant zealots in his government, he ordered seizure of the lands of the old church, which entailed dissolution of all the monasteries of England, many of them ancient. Over about 6 years, a grand appropriation took place but the Crown's bounty did not last long. Henry needed money and even

---

[3] By the mid-1530s, the royal coffers were depleted by earlier wasteful wars with France, and court expenditure. Henry needed money, and influenced by his Lord Chancellor, Thomas Cromwell, a Protestant who wanted to demolish the apparatus of the Catholic Church, he decided to dissolve all monasteries in England.

while dissolution continued, he began to sell appropriated land to gentry and nobility.

In doing so, he effected an extraordinary transfer of property, creating in the old nobility and the middle-class magnates,[4] landowners on a great scale, who could also expect to wield political power. Dissolution consolidated the Crown's power, and made irreversible the shift towards Protestantism of the middle classes and nobility. As beneficiaries of the Crown's appropriation, they gained too much from apostasy to consider anything other than collaboration with the king.

By the time of Henry's death in 1547, all the radical developments in Europe over the previous 200 years, the spread of humanism, the Black Death, the explosion of printing, the Protestant Reformation, were identifiable as the harbingers of a new age in which the individual looked to self, not heaven, to determine action, turned away from doctrine and regarded expedience as a virtue. In the new era, a well-organized collective of printers could position itself to harness the winds of change, and, like the new magnates of property and enterprise, seize the benefits of royal favour.

3.7 Lobbying for Monopoly

The dissolution of the monasteries, a shocking event for most ordinary English people, and the cause of bewilderment and anger, especially in the countryside, worked in favour of the Stationers' Company. Hankering for print monopoly, they took note of Henry's evident alarm at opposition to his actions and waited for the opportunity to impress the king with their capacity to efficiently censor dangerous literature.

In 1536, Henry's attack on the old church provoked a northern uprising, the Pilgrimage of Grace, which he suppressed with a combination of duplicity and brutality. Thereafter, in the final decade of his life, he grew steadily more alarmed at perceived threats to his authority. His paranoia strengthened the grip of his censors. In 1538—the mid-point in the campaigns against the monasteries—he banned, by royal decree, the printing of any book in English without the authorization of a Privy Councillor. Censorship became a central element of policy and the infamous Star Chamber the guardian of conformity.

In 1542, the Stationers asked the king to approve a charter that would empower their corporation to license—on behalf of the Crown—the printing of all books in England. Henry declined to delegate the task of censorship, or to agree a second request, that only guild members be licensed to print books.[5] But the Stationers

[4] Some of the wealthy beneficiaries of Henry's policy, like a considerable number of gentry of more modest means, embraced religious non-conformism and their descendants contributed to the ranks of the parliamentary party that, a 100 years later, fought the Civil War against King Charles.

[5] He drafted a proclamation that, among other things, required the destruction of proscribed texts, and prohibited the importation, without royal licence, of books in English printed abroad.

were not deterred. They had lobbied the Crown for exclusive printing privileges for over 30 years and they continued to do so after the king's death in 1547.

After Henry, who maintained a religious policy of uneasy accommodation, the battle between Catholics and Protestants for political supremacy began to reach fever pitch. The Stationers' promise to efficiently carry out the task of censorship became attractive to the King's successors, Edward and Mary, each of whom struggled to enforce opposite policies, one in favour of Protestantism, the other Catholicism. After another decade of endeavour, the Stationers received their reward.

In 1557, Queen Mary issued a Charter which, though it reserved to the Crown the right to issue printing patents to individual petitioners, gave the corporation responsibility for licensing the printing of publications in any part of England. The Stationers policed themselves, for only members of their Company could print works. Printing could not take place without registration, a rule that enabled the corporation to choke the supply of any material regarded as seditious or dangerous by government or ecclesiastical authorities.

3.8 The Stationers' Monopoly

Stationers' copyright, subject to internal approval procedures, automatically applied to material printed by a member of the Stationers' Company. Publication depended on registration and since the Stationers were solely responsible for registration, they controlled the publication of all books. After 1557, the printing trade concentrated in London.

Patent copyright offered a limited monopoly, lasting for a specified number of years. But Stationers' copyright, conferred by registration, lasted indefinitely and thus a Stationer who registered a book enjoyed monopoly printing rights for as long as he lived. It took only a few steps of logic for booksellers in the eighteenth century to assert that the Stationers' copyright lasted forever, and that the statutory term of copyright could not extinguish this eternal 'common law copyright'.

The Stationers are principal actors in the story of statutory copyright. Their monopoly control of printing and publication determined the way in which lawyers defined literary property in the eighteenth century. Until the later transformation of copyright into sets of extensive exclusive rights, the copyright holder possessed the same privilege as that secured by the Stationers: the exclusive right to print and publish a book.

The Stationers established a pattern of lobbying for advantages imitated ever since by those seeking exclusive rights. They were models of the astute businessmen who have dominated the history of copyright law-making. Above all, they were pragmatic and flexible. They arranged the suppression of books, and accepted with equanimity the changing fashion that asked them to first proscribe Protestant literature, and then Catholic, later Calvinist, then Anglican.[6]

[6] The Long Parliament, convened in 1640 by the financially desperate King Charles I, abolished the Star Chamber and its licensing decree of 1637, which had reduced the number of licensed

During the Civil War in the seventeenth century, they smoothly changed sides as the fortunes of King and Parliament ebbed and flowed, and they welcomed the restoration of monarchy as if they never knew the regicides to whom they were allied. They were, in short, the first in a long line of cabals that, into the present day, have won government approval to control the supply of information on terms that suit their business interests.[7]

Like all cabals, they created a plentiful supply of enemies. No less a figure than the philosopher John Locke wrote a memorandum in 1695 against licensing, the year that parliament declined to renew the licensing law. Despite the Stationers' entreaties over the next few years, the legislature refused to reinstate their privilege.

Reference

Clark K (1972) Civilisation. BBC/John Murray, London

printers to 23 and increased the severity of penalties. Political and religious controversy now flourished. In 2 years the number of pamphlets printed grew from about 22 to nearly 2,000. Civil war broke out in 1642 and in 1643, parliament, fearful of criticism, reinstated licensing. In 1644, the poet John Milton published *The Areopagitica*, a tract notable for its bigotry towards the Catholic faith but also famous for its argument that censorship degrades rather than protects society. Dr Samuel Johnson, who wrote an unflattering biography of the poet, expressed scepticism about Milton's enthusiasm for liberty: 'they who clamour most loudly for liberty do not most liberally grant it'.

[7] King Charles II reinstituted licensing of literature in 1662, and though the practice lapsed, his successor James II passed a new licensing Act in 1685. Parliament renewed the Act in 1692 for 2 years, then refused to do so again in 1694. The monopoly over printing vanished and the Stationers contended, often successfully, with competitors.

Chapter 4
The Eighteenth Century: Liberty and Literary Property: Statutory Copyright

4.1 The Statute of Anne

The passing of the Statute of Anne in 1710 is often identified as the seminal moment in copyright history. For the first time, legislation recognized an author's—not bookseller's—right to control the reproduction of books. The author's copyright—the exclusive right to control copying of books—lasted for a period of 14 years from publication and could, on expiry, be renewed by the author for a second 14-year term.[1] By recognizing the author's right to property in books 'and Writings',[2] the Statute of Anne laid the foundation for the modern edifice of copyright regulation.[3]

The Act also resolved long-standing antagonism between publishers and parliamentarians, many of whom wanted to drive a dagger through the heart of the booksellers' monopoly. Parliament's dislike of the Stationers' Company could be dated to at least the Civil War and possibly long before,[4] and after the so-called

[1] The Act stated that the Stationers' copyright in books continued for another 21 years.

[2] References to 'other Writings' occurred only once, in the opening paragraph of the operative part of the Act. The remainder of the Act referred only to 'Books'. The drafter may have used the term 'other Writings' as a convenient catch-all phrase designating pamphlets, posters and similar popular forms of printed material. The phrase might also indicate early understanding that literary property vested in an abstract 'work' rather than a physical 'book'. On the other hand, parliamentary drafters in the United Kingdom only ceased to tie literary property to 'a Book' in 1911, when new copyright legislation adopted the categories of copyright works.

[3] Although the grant to the Stationers' Company recognized a power to make copies, thus establishing a formal copyright, the Stationers' rights related to the printing of books, not the content of the books. The Statute of Anne established, explicitly, copyright in the book, although it did not refer to copyright in the intangible elements of the book—what later came to be known as the 'literary work'.

[4] In 1655, Oliver Cromwell limited the company's powers in favour of a Council of State. However, in 1623, the Statute of Monopolies, which abolished monopolies in England subject to broad exceptions (applying to certain kinds of 'new manufactures' or monopolies granted to corporations, companies and so on), did not remove the Stationers' exclusive rights.

B. Atkinson and B. Fitzgerald, *A Short History of Copyright*,
DOI 10.1007/978-3-319-02075-4_4, © Springer International Publishing Switzerland 2014

'Glorious Revolution' of 1688 ushered in constitutional monarchy, law-makers renewed the attack on old privileges granted by the Crown.

Historically opposed to the arbitrary exercise of the royal prerogative, the legislature had hunted down royal privileges for 75 years. Perhaps mindful that its 2-year experiment in print freedom ended in puritan suppression in 1643, and careful to maintain peace with Charles II, parliament did not, during the Restoration, rush to kill the monopoly that traditionally it regarded as most odious. However, by 1694, closing on a century spent in degrees of conflict with the English Crown, parliament, or at least many of its members, felt viscerally hostile to royal decrees they thought to be emanations of capricious individual will. Like the American revolutionaries 60 or more years later, they came to view Crown fiats as tyrannical, proof that undiluted authority is inevitably bad.

The Stationers' monopoly, and the censorship that accompanied it, stood out in the thicket of old royal decrees, exemplifying to many the Crown's abuse of power. Politicians saw the need for continuing action, and the Statute of Anne, redressing past injustices against authors and suborning copyright to the noble task of spreading knowledge, expressed their activism. Much later, after the success of the constitutional settlement exorcised from parliamentary minds the spectre of royal tyranny, nature resumed its ordinary course, and parliaments conferred many copyright monopolies.[5]

The initiative for copyright legislation cannot be assigned to one person or faction. It grew from the hybrid wishes of publishers, especially the old Stationers, who wanted regulation of a chaotic market, and politicians, who wanted to strike at monopoly. In its final form, the legislation could not be characterized as friendly to the booksellers. It worked in their favour, but its contents revealed a more permissive attitude to the control of information than is usually attributed to copyright legislators.

The wish for a liberal publishing regime leading to more production, and more competition, provoked a reaction. To the extent that the legislators wished to create a commercial market favourable to the dissemination of knowledge, they strengthened the impetus among the chief booksellers to press for laws that would concentrate in their hands control over dissemination.[6]

[5] Parliament's hostility to monopolies at the time of the Statute of Anne was real but can be overstated. Most parliamentarians disliked the arbitrary exercise of royal power. However, in the first seven decades of the eighteenth century, Parliament did not prevent the grant of a number of royal privileges to music publishers.

[6] Though the booksellers correctly interpreted the prevailing political sentiment against any cause associated with the Stationers they lobbied hardest for legislation, and in 1709, arranged for their supporters to submit a bill drafted to remedy the damage done by unauthorized reprints to 'the Properties' of 'Proprietors' and the 'Discouragement of all Writers'. The first draft of the bill did not limit the duration of copyright. Identification with the cause of 'writers' positioned booksellers to secure legislation that in substance favoured them.

4.2 Support for Dissemination

Copyright legislative history since the Stationers' Charter of 1557 tells a story of information repression, but in 1710, parliamentarians made explicit their desire for copyright law to encourage the spread of knowledge. The Act's preamble declared the purpose of the legislation to be 'the Encouragement of Learning'. A few lines later, the statute enlarged on this intention, declaring that it was enacted 'for the encouragement of Learned Men to compose and write useful Books'.

For good measure, the Act made clear parliament's opinion of the booksellers:

> Whereas Printers, Booksellers, and other Persons have of late frequently taken the Liberty of Printing, Reprinting, and Publishing, or causing to be Printed, Reprinted, and Published Books, and other Writings, without the Consent of the Authors or Proprietors of such Books and Writings, to their very great Detriment, and too often to the ruin of them and their Families: For Preventing, therefore such Practices for the future.

The specification of a maximum copyright term of 28 years also struck at the booksellers. By providing useful service to the Crown as the licensor of books, the Stationers' Company forestalled, over many years, concerns about the duration of its printing monopoly. The Crown seemed implicitly to accept the Stationers' assertions that the charter conferred perpetual monopoly. The Statute of Anne, however, rejected the idea of perpetual copyright. That it did so unequivocally did not stop the booksellers, over 50 years later, from arguing passionately before receptive judges that statute could not extinguish something conferred by nature as a permanent gift: so-called common law copyright.

4.3 Perpetual Copyright

Cast out of the Eden of market control, the Stationers' and their competitors looked for ways to recreate the ideal world of never-ending copyright. For many years after the enactment of the Statute of Anne, booksellers, their ranks swollen by the astute Scottish publishers concentrated in Edinburgh, fought each other tooth and nail for shares of an ever-growing market. Demand boomed against a background of national confidence and political unity.

The 1707 Act of Union had joined the parliaments of England and Scotland, and the people of each country, already united under a single monarch, became citizens of one political entity, the United Kingdom. They now participated in a common market. Political stability and the expansion of commerce in the unified kingdom stimulated the taste for literature and the production of books.

If the booksellers were ordinary merchants, they would have rejoiced in a time of plenty. But like the dispossessed aristocrats of a later era, scheming to reclaim their lost estates, they were obsessed with recovering the magical endowment of perpetual copyright. That this gift had belonged only to the Stationers did not reduce their enthusiasm. For the booksellers, the right to eternal copyright was no less the province of natural law than the parliamentarians' claim to liberty.

Why they thought in this way is not rationally explicable. The 28-year copyright term did not harm the book trade. Very few books fetch buyers 5 years after publication, let alone 28. A perpetual term, while useful to the beneficiaries of copyright in those rare books for which demand never fails, was of nil present value to the booksellers. Nor did the booksellers contend with an aggressive band of authors driving hard bargains and eating into their margins. The idea of authors winning much more than fame or repute from their books, though gestating, could hardly be said to be a predominant factor in the publishers' pecuniary calculations.

Emotion seems to have distorted the mental processes of these hard men of business. Even though most booksellers appeared on the scene after the Stationers' monopoly ended, they shared the Stationers' devotion to the principle that publishing rights belonged to the holder forever—even though they must have realized that perpetual copyright offered none of them an everlasting material benefit, or even benefit for a lifetime. Thus for many years they pressed for legislative change and eventually turned to the courts to achieve their objectives. Along the way, they supported their case with arguments familiar to today's observer of arguments for extension to the copyright term.

The 28-year term, they said, drove many to the wall because, given piracy of books, they could never recover investment costs within so limited a timeframe. Such a short term ended businesses and beggared families. The argument, though nonsensical—no bookseller, or proprietor of any business, could afford to plan for recovering investments in a period so long as 28 years—gained ground, and contributed to perceptions that the Statute of Anne somehow disentitled publishers.

The publishers argued for perpetual copyright in a string of cases beginning in 1750 (*Millar* v. *Kinkaid*[7]) and ending in 1774 in *Donaldson* v. *Beckett*.[8] In *Millar* v. *Taylor* (1769), they seemed to have won a decisive victory but in *Donaldson*, the House of Lords turned its back on their claims. In the end, the support of two luminaries of English law, Lord Mansfield and William Blackstone, the former presiding over the King's Bench in *Millar* v. *Taylor* and the latter a judge in *Donaldson*, could not rescue their cause.

Mansfield and Blackstone relied on John Locke's labour theory to assert natural rights as the basis for common law copyright inextinguishable by statute.[9] However, in *Donaldson*, Lord Camden responded to the booksellers' arguments with withering scorn, and the Lords voted 6:5 that even if common law copyright existed, the Statute of Anne extinguished it.

The Lords accepted the argument of Attorney General Thurlow that a literary work is 'beyond the comprehension of man's understanding and hardly capable of

[7] 98 ER 210.

[8] 28 Eng Rep 257.

[9] Locke, in Chapter 5 of the second of his *Two Treatises on Government* (1689/1988) argued that man by his labour annexes what he produces. The fruit of his labour is his private property.

being defined'. No fixed relationship existed between the printed word and the formulations of the mind. The authors' thoughts were, in the earlier words of Justice Yates,[10] 'phantoms', and the printed page neither possessed nor annexed them. Copyright could not vest in something indefinable that existed once and for all in the author's mind. Nature had not decreed that authors created eternal property. Copyright existed because statute granted, for a limited time, the right to produce copies of books.

So, seemingly, ended the booksellers' charge towards a monopoly that would have meant that the copyright in published books never lapsed.[11]

4.4 Ideas of Liberty

The Renaissance (c late thirteenth to sixteenth centuries), Reformation (c sixteenth to seventeenth centuries) and Enlightenment (c seventeenth to eighteenth centuries) asserted in principle the primacy of individual human decision in matters of faith, morals or social action. By identifying the power of personal agency to effect personal or collective improvement, these movements, though philosophically disparate,[12] presaged creation of new political systems in Europe and the United States.

Arguments for political freedom, diverse, complex, rent and shaped the politics of Europe, and later North America, between the sixteenth and eighteenth centuries (and world politics in succeeding centuries).[13] From contention, strife and war

---

[10] *Millar* v. *Taylor* (1769).

[11] For detailed treatment of the debate and litigation over perpetual copyright, see Rose (1994), Bently and Sherman (1999), and Deazley (2004).

[12] Individual autonomy characterises each of these three movements. The intellectual origins of Reformation are to some degree traceable to the German Renaissance (c fifteenth century), which interpreted, again by degree, the humanism of the Italian Renaissance. Similarly, it could reasonably be argued that the Enlightenment could not have taken place had the Reformation not occurred (a representative presentation of this argument is given by Russell 1946). Philosophically, they are remotely connected. The humanism of the Italian Renaissance, inspired by Greco-Roman culture of antiquity, sought to liberate human reason and capabilities from constraints of conformity and obedience, but it did not reject natural law or revelation, nor the transcendental, sublime or mystical aspects of art and literature. The Reformation opposed religious authority and tradition, and an allied culture that profusely explored sacred and human themes. Beginning with Martin Luther (d. 1546), Reformation leaders established the formulae of 'faith alone' and 'by scripture alone', which in theory permitted individual believers to discern religious truth independently of authorities propagating doctrine. The Enlightenment, by contrast, divorced itself from belief, or revelation, and asserted that by application of their reason humans could come to discern reality and understand how to improve their conditions of life.

[13] In Europe, the dimensions of the Reformation movement began to change. The Reformation transformed from a religious protest into a political cause, co-opted by princes and electors to achieve secession, gain territory, or procure temporal advantages. The Protestant religious program (Calvinist as well as Lutheran) thus formed a backdrop to both internecine state conflicts and

emerged principles of toleration, representation and freedom from oppression. These principles were elaborated from the premise, which remains the premise of the modern idea of equality, that personhood, by itself, confers on each person certain identical rights, which must every just polity must recognise.[14]

Philosophers and propagandists of liberty, including Thomas Hobbes (d. 1679), John Locke (d. 1704), Montesquieu (d. 1755),[15] Voltaire (d. 1778),[16] Jean-Jaques Rousseau (d. 1778), Denis Diderot (d. 1784) and Immanuel Kant (d. 1804) advanced ideas about human freedom. People must be left free, according to the principle of liberty, to think and do as they please.[17] The idea of liberty is a political idea, and the English Parliament promulgated the first national statement of political liberty in 1689, passing the Bill of Rights.[18]

Practical admirers of various Enlightenment philosophers, most notably the authors and inheritors of the American and French revolutions (beginning 1775 and 1789) debated what limits to place on liberty, and the type of political system that might guarantee its continued existence.[19] From their deliberations emerged a

---

those involving multiple states. Conflict in western Europe began before Luther's death in 1546, closed temporarily in 1555 (Peace of Augsburg), continued fitfully in the later part of the sixteenth century, then erupted in 1618 in a war of Empire and states. This war, brought to an end by the Peace of Westphalia in 1648, consumed a large part of central and western Europe. Its ending weakened the power of the Hapsburg Empire, especially in Germanic territories, and increased the influence of France. It confirmed also the independence of the Netherlands from its former imperial master, Spain. So began the era of nation states, but more significantly, so far as developments concerning social equality are concerned, the Treaty of Westphalia introduced a principle of religious toleration, allowing non-conforming citizens of Catholic, Lutheran or Calvinist states freedom of religious practice. It marked the end of wars in Europe involving primary dispute over religion.

[14] In short, the philosophy of liberty, which is not a doctrine but a kind of syllabus of different writings and documents, especially those of the seventeenth to eighteenth centuries, reaching apotheosis, though not finality, in the declarations of independence promulgated during the revolutions of the United States and France (1776 and 1793). The philosophy of liberty locates sovereignty in the collective of people ruled by law, and determines that sovereignty is the consequence of each qualified person's native endowment as free and equal. Each person possesses the same sovereign right to determine government in a polity. Thus the only legitimate government or law is one that gives effect to the expressed will of qualified persons acting together to select, directly or by proxy, executive, parliament and judiciary.

[15] Charles-Louis de Secondat, Baron de La Brède et Montesquieu.

[16] François-Marie Arouet.

[17] Or as John Locke explained (*Two Treatises of Government*, 1689/1988) a person's rights to life, property and individual liberty is inviolate by reason of natural law, and natural rights are not to be abrogated by coercion. A government must protect these rights, and is legitimate to the extent that it does so; its continuation must be by popular consent.

[18] The Bill transferred from crown to parliament asserted or residual political power of the monarch, although the crown remained the source of state power.

[19] For an account of how leading Enlightenment figures differed in interpreting ideas of universal liberty, and equality without distinction, see Siep Stuurman 'Global Equality and Inequality in Enlightenment Thought' *Reeks Burgerhartlezingen Werkgroep 18e Eeuw nummer 3* Burgerhart Lecture 2010.

political principle of equality, and a political conception of inequality, usually secular, though not always.[20]

The United States Declaration of Independence (1776) declared that, '... all men are created equal ... endowed by their Creator with certain inalienable rights ...'. The French Revolutionary Declaration of the Rights of Man and the Citizen (1793) stated that 'Men are born and remain free and equal in rights. Social distinctions may be founded only upon the general good.'

Ideas of freedom, translated by some into licence to appropriate, and in any case, expressed in the language of individual rights, shaped societies receptive to copyright principles. Societies in the vanguard of innovation embraced the idea that endless scientific discovery and invention promised unending progress to a future of increasing material welfare. Ideals of liberty could readily be reconciled with ideas of progress since political freedom is a much better guarantor of capital and profits than political restriction.

4.5 Developments in the United States

In the last quarter of the eighteenth century, extraordinary changes remade the politics and society of the European and North American worlds. Liberalism began its long march as a political creed, and the American and French revolutions entranced admirers with the vision of free society that encourages the best human impulses.

Britain became the world's foremost military and economic power, although the two great revolutionary nations saw in its empire and politics reaction and oppression. Its parliament had long cast off the vice of royal veto, and could boast two unique developments, the party political and cabinet systems. Political toleration (which applied only to Protestants) helped to emancipate forces of invention and materialism, and they unleashed the Industrial Revolution, transforming Britain and the world.

In the United Kingdom, change encouraged the publishers to tie themselves more zealously to the masthead of official policy. Where their nation went, creating possessions and colonies, so did they, establishing markets over which governments increasingly granted them monopoly control. Domestically, they carried on selling books in a market regulated by the Statute of Anne. Economic growth and the emergence of industrial cities increased the number of consumers and the diversity of demand. Many publishers, though they never gave up the dream of perpetual copyright, became regulatory conservatives.

[20] One of the most famous contemporary advocates of universal equality, Guillaume Raynal ('Abbé Raynal' d 1796) in the bestselling *L'Histoire philosophique et politique des établissements et du commerce des Européens dans les deux Indes* ('Philosophical and Political History of European Possessions and Trade in the Two Indies' 1770) affirmed that all men are, without qualification, equal 'in the eyes of the Supreme Being.'

Across the Atlantic, however, the forging of the United States in the white heat of revolution made conservatism impossible. Final victory over the British at Yorktown in 1781 came 3 years after the ratification of the world's first and greatest national constitution, a document that swept away the possibility of tyranny. The United States Constitution expressed the extraordinary spirit and daring of the revolutionaries. Their leaders rebelled against the arbitrary claims and exactions of a faraway parliament that offered the American colonies no voice. When they cast off British oppression, they wanted no more of capricious authority justified by privilege.

Thomas Jefferson translated hostility to unrepresentative government into positive sentiments that influenced the growth in the United States of a *purposive* attitude to copyright law. The Declaration of Independence in 1776 declared that:

> We hold these truths to be self-evident, that all men are created equal, that they are endowed by their creator with certain inalienable Rights, that among these are Life, Liberty and the pursuit of Happiness.

Inspired by this affirmation, the framers of the constitution drafted a copyright clause, Article I, Section 8, granting Congress power to:

> promote the Progress of Science and useful Arts, by securing for limited Times to Authors and Inventors the exclusive Right to their respective Writings and Discoveries.

In stark contrast to the Stationers' Charter, which launched their long monopoly, the copyright clause implicitly identified public welfare as the goal of copyright legislation. Who other than citizens stood to benefit from the progress of science and useful arts?

In 1791, a bill of rights incorporated in the Constitution 10 amendments, the first of which materially affected the development of United States copyright law. The First Amendment stated that, 'Congress shall make no law respecting the establishment of religion, or prohibiting the free exercise thereof; or abridging the freedom of speech, or of the press.' Read together, the copyright clause and First Amendment invited the observer to view American copyright as a restricted privilege, one that could not be utilized to censor books—and the opposite of the Stationers' monopoly, which constitutionalists like Jefferson considered corrupt in origin and purpose.[21]

4.6 Pre-union

The question of copyright had arisen in the colonies 3 years before the Declaration of Independence. Until the Revolution, American colonists do not appear to have been much exercised by questions of literary property. In economies that afford for

[21] For modern case discussion of the effect of the copyright clause, see, for example, *Harper & Row* v. *Nation Enterprises*, 471 US 539 (1985) and *Eldred* v. *Ashcroft* 537 US 186 (2003).

most people restricted opportunity for leisure or learning the protection of literature is not an uppermost concern.

For much of the eighteenth century, energies were diverted away from authorship. Could the Statute of Anne have regulated the colonies, it would have functioned, as did imperial legislation in the nineteenth century, to secure for British publishers control over colonial trade in books. Had imperial legislation applied to eighteenth century American colonies, British trade monopoly could only have stoked revolutionary flames.

It may be that in the early part of the eighteenth century, British parliamentarians were little concerned by publishing across the Atlantic. If their forebears were not greatly moved by literary matters, by the time of the Revolution, a time of pamphlets and manifestos, few Americans would have doubted the power of literature. In 1783, the Continental Congress encouraged states to pass legislation granting copyright to authors for a term similar to that in the Statute of Anne, 14 years, renewable on expiry. By 1786, all states but one had passed legislation (three had done so before 1783).

4.7 The Copyright Act 1790

From his distant post as Minister to France, in the years 1788–1789, Thomas Jefferson corresponded with James Madison, principal author of the Constitution and Bill of Rights, and a member of Congress from 1789, on questions of monopoly and copyright. Jefferson and Madison were later political allies and both held the offices of secretary of state and president.

On the question of proprietary rights they held different opinions. Madison supported legislation to establish copyright and patents while Jefferson, though not categorically opposed to Madison's programme, keenly pointed out his dislike of government-sanctioned monopolies. Jefferson maintained his interest in the subject: his last correspondence concerning monopoly rights is dated 1813.

In any case, copyright legislation supported by Madison and passed in 1790,[22] settled, for practical purposes, any controversy between them. Whatever his feelings on the subject, Jefferson could not prevent from Paris the enactment of legislation that created an exclusive copyright lasting for the same period as the term in the Statute of Anne—14 years, renewable for another 14 years if the author survived the first term.

It is easy to overstate Jefferson's opposition to the legislation. His letters on the subject of copyright or monopoly are, over a period of 25 years, principally

[22] Copyright Act 1790, *An Act for the Encouragement of Learning, by securing the Copies of Maps, Charts and Books, to the Authors and Proprietors of such Copies, during the Times therein mentioned.*

concerned with pointing out the dangers of granting rights that encourage commercial oppression or abuse, to the public detriment.[23]

But he supported measures that encouraged invention and creativeness. The 1790 Copyright Act, like the Statue of Anne on which it was partly based, declared its primary purpose to be a public one: that of encouraging learning. American legislators, spokesmen for freedom of thought and expression, wanted copyright law to be a means of encouraging the dissemination of ideas and knowledge. They saw no need to depart from the 80-year-old formula, albeit stated in a British statute, for securing the benefit of author and public.

In reality, both British and US statutes played into the hands of publishers who, whether by direct assignment or contractual stipulation, controlled the author's copyright and dictated the terms of supply to the public. The publishers looked disdainfully at enactments that ostensibly limited their power, and they maintained their claim for perpetual copyright. In substance, they won the victory. The discourse of natural rights, so evident in the publishers' arguments in *Millar* and *Donaldson*, eventually persuaded jurists and legislators in the United States to turn their backs on Jefferson's declarations against monopoly power.

Legislation in 1831 and 1909 extended the duration of US copyright to a possible period of 42 and 56 years from publication, and in 1976 and 1998 increased the term to posthumous periods of 50 and 70 years. When Jefferson proposed a copyright term of 19 years (the average period of life remaining to members of the US population in 1790) he pointed out that '*the earth belongs in usufruct to the living*: that the dead have neither powers nor rights over it'.[24] He probably did not consider the possibility of the United States legislature providing for posthumous terms of such length that, for practical purposes, the duration of copyright might as well be stated to be infinite.

4.8 Statute Defines Copyright

With Jefferson's practical views on copyright's purpose and length, the early Supreme Court agreed, and it rejected the argument that nature decreed authors' rights. Copyright statutes in no way uncovered parts of a hypothesized natural law, rather they positively stated all the rights relating to the subject. In *Wheaton* v. *Peters* (1834), the Supreme Court accepted the reasoning in *Donaldson* and declared that a perpetual term could not be inferred from the supposed natural law. Unequivocally, statute defined the entirety of rights available to the copyright holder.[25]

---

[23] For representative letters, see Atkinson and Fitzgerald (2011), pp. 245–261.

[24] Letter to James Madison, 6 September 1789 (see Atkinson and Fitzgerald 2011).

[25] The case concerned the suit of Wheaton, the Supreme Court's Reporter of Decisions. Wheaton compiled reports of the court's decisions together with case notes and received income from the

The Act of 1790 did, however, depart from the Statute of Anne in two important respects. First, it applied to maps and charts as well as books. Later legislation added engravings, etchings and prints (1802), 'music' and 'cuts' (1831),[26] and by 1871 the panoply included dramatic or musical compositions, paintings, drawings, chromo, statutes, statuary, photographs, negatives and fine art models or designs. Already, Congress contemplated that copyright law would move beyond the realm of books and publishers and extend to fields that were related only to the extent that output involved multiple copying, and the exposure of copies for sale (an act the law recognized as a species of publication).

Second, the United States legislation recognized the copyright only of American citizens or residents. Foreigners could not obtain legal redress in the United States courts. In the nineteenth century in Europe, many countries accorded foreign copyright holders the right to sue under domestic copyright law. US practice created a highly lucrative publishing industry in the nineteenth century that thrived on pirating books published in the United Kingdom and selling them to the burgeoning US market at a fraction of the British retail price. British authors, including Charles Dickens, protested against US piracy in vain. When Dickens, during a reading tour of the United States in 1841, spoke against the practice of American publishers, a hostile press attacked him.[27]

These innovations pointed to a future in which copyright became the chosen regulatory instrument of industries seeking monopoly rights, and the rubric of an international system that enforced those rights. Ironically, the piracy that international treaties helped partly to preclude, and for which the US became infamous in the nineteenth century, became, towards the end of the twentieth century and beyond, a central focus of international copyright law-makers led by the United States.

4.9 France and Moral Rights

Enacted near the beginning and end of the eighteenth century, the Statute of Anne and the US Copyright Act struck at privilege, and the political absolutism from which privilege sprang. Although each granted monopoly rights of relatively short

---

sale of volumes compiled. His successor, Peters, continued to compile reports and he abridged for sale Wheaton's earlier texts. The cheaper abridged versions outsold Wheaton's original texts and Wheaton sued Peters for copyright infringement. However, Wheaton had not fulfilled registration formalities required by the copyright legislation and the Court denied his putative copyright. The Court ruled that the statute, and not rights implied from natural law, determined the legal issues.

[26] In the equivalent period leading into the 1830s, the UK passed the Sculpture Act 1833 and the Dramatic Copyright Act 1833.

[27] The poet Walt Whitman, then a Manhattan newspaper editor, to pour scorn on Dickens, published a derogatory letter about the United States presented to suggest it came from Dickens. For detailed consideration of Whitman's attitude to copyright, see Buinicki (2003).

duration, they did so only in part to advantage authors. Legislators wanted principally to benefit the public, or at least that part of the public with time and income to spend on books. They did not waste much time thinking about the welfare of the common herd. Most thought of the public not as the plurality of citizens but rather as victims of the Crown's unjust exercise of authority.

The United States Act, of course, emerged from the creative swirl of great events, and the deliberations of one of the greatest legislative assemblies ever gathered. Its arrival coincided with the beginning of the French Revolution, which, in a few years, would bring forth the horrors of dictatorship by committee, and state-sponsored murder, as well as copyright legislation born of a philosophy distinct from that which inspired the British and US codes.

Pragmatism characterized the legislation of the English-speaking countries, although the political innovations of the United States far outstripped the British parliament's gradual extension of political liberties. Nothing written in England by 1710 could in any degree match the declarative ambition and force of the *Declaration of Independence* or the US Constitution.

By asserting humanity's permanent entitlement to political freedom these documents promised an attitude to social development outside the understanding of politicians in the United Kingdom. Even so, copyright legislation in the United Kingdom and the United States, while to some extent philosophically charged, was the product of social equilibrium. Allowing for the application of the First Amendment to the United States Act, and the publicly minded sentiment of the constitutional copyright power, both reflect pragmatism and common sense rather than revolutionary ambition.

The same is not true of the copyright decree of the French National Convention issued on 19 July 1793.[28] The decree of 1793, though remarkably short (consisting of seven provisions), proved durable, lasting through the nineteenth century. It established property in literary and artistic works. The formal elaboration of moral rights, the droit moral, would await the exhaustion of controversies in the nineteenth century, and the consensus that emerged later in that century when Victor Hugo led the movement for recognition of authors' rights. But the idea of droit moral entered the French consciousness from an early date.

The French Revolution began in 1789, and through succeeding political vicissitudes lasting into the twentieth century, the French population absorbed and accepted the message of natural rights contained in the *Declaration of the Rights of Man and the Citizen* adopted at the outset of revolution. 'Men are born and remain free and equal in rights', announced the declaration, and the proponents of authors' rights took to heart the message that humans lie at the centre of creation. Their genius deserved the law's protection and the compact between author and

[28] *Décret de la Convention Nationale du dix-neuf juillet 1793 relatif aux droits de propriété des Auteurs d'écrits en tout genre, des Compositeurs de musique, des Peintres et des Dessinateurs (avec le rapport de Lakanal)* or Decree of the National Convention, of 19 July 1793, concerning authors' property rights in all types of writing and the rights in their work of composers of music, painters and illustrators.

code took precedence over the material concerns of the investors—publishers—who made possible for authors another compact, with the book purchasing public.

Authors, according to the droit moral, deserved to be identified and expect that copies would not subtract from literary integrity of works. Shortly before Napoleon embarked unregenerate on the path of mayhem and disaster, he commissioned rational laws to govern civil society. The Napoleonic Code (1805) set a precedent for civil law-makers everywhere. As ideas of droit moral infiltrated French legal thinking, so they also spread across the globe. In non-English-speaking countries, many drafters of copyright codes adopted French ideas about copyright.

In the civil law countries apologists did not struggle to justify copyrights, and in those jurisdictions, the author occupied the central place in the process of production. The common-sense tradition of English-speaking countries did not so readily accord special status to authors. Few citizens of either the United States or the United Kingdom believed that nature decreed authors to be a privileged class of human beings, and their legislatures did not depart from the principle that any privilege granted to authors must be justified by its public utility.

Increasingly, however, confusion crept into the copyright discourse of the English-speaking nations. Utilitarian laws in favour of limited copyright monopolies were reinterpreted by the proponents of authors' rights as the expression of natural law. Thus began the long argument between those who declared the laws were intended to benefit the public, and those who said they arose to protect the inalienable rights of authors.

4.10 Copyright Works

Until the Berne Convention's normative leap—near the close of the nineteenth century—in favour of authors' rights, principles of copyright regulation usually concerned the production (and distribution) of books, and the exercise of the dramatic or musical performing rights. But in Germany at the end of the eighteenth century, two philosophers prepared the ground for the Berne Union to extend copyright protection to different categories of expressive works.

Johann Gottlieb Fichte, an originator of German idealism, distinguished between the object and its essence, creating a distinction that underpinned the later differentiation between a book and a work. Referring to books, he stated that the author's locutions are the *form* of the author's ideas, and his literary property. The ideas expressed, separate from form, are not the subject of property.[29]

Immanuel Kant, the greatest German philosopher of the eighteenth century, pointed to the distinct identity of works created from literary endeavour. Kant

[29] See, e.g., brief focused discussion and material collected by Karl-Erik Tallmo at www.copyrighthistory.com.

identified the author's interest with his identity or 'person', his observations precursors to arguments for moral rights.

Both men appeared to be aware of the controversies over literary property in England earlier in the century. Both discussed the difference between what Fichte called the physical nature of book and its *intellectual* content. Fichte's contemporary, another great German idealist, Georg Wilhelm Friedrich Hegel, also commented on how 'inward and mental' objects could be alienated for legal purposes. An author's work, said Hegel, expressed the self or 'will' and this selfhood could not be appropriated by another. For that reason, a person could buy a book but not copy it because the selfhood expressed in the work is governed by the author.[30]

German idealism permeated legal thinking slowly but in time the distinction between things and essence allowed for the formulation for which the booksellers and their supporters had searched in vain in the middle of the eighteenth century: that which distinguished between corporeal objects like books and *works*, the incorporeal subject matter of those books. Although the idealists seemingly did not otherwise turn their minds to questions of book regulation, and the regulators paid little heed to idealism, in time, philosophical developments in late eighteenth-century Germany proved fruitful in the growth of copyright law.

References

Atkinson B, Fitzgerald B (eds) (2011) The library of essays on copyright. Ashgate, Farnham, pp 245–261

Bently L, Sherman B (1999) The making of modern intellectual property law. Cambridge University Press, Cambridge

Buinicki MT (2003) Walt Whitman and the question of copyright. Am Lit Hist 15(2):248–275

Deazley R (2004) On the origin of the right to copy – charting the movement of copyright law in eighteenth-century Britain (1695–1775). Hart, Oxford

Hegel GWF (1821/1991) Elements of the philosophy of right (Grundlinien der Philosophie des Rechts). Cambridge, Berlin

Locke J (1689/1988) Two treatises of government. Cambridge University Press, Cambridge

Rose M (1994) Owners and authors: the invention of copyright. Harvard University Press, Cambridge

Russell B (1946) A history of western philosophy. Allen & Unwin, London

[30] See Hegel (1821/1991).

Chapter 5
The Nineteenth Century: Liberty and Literary Property

5.1 The Nineteenth Century

The first half of the nineteenth century witnessed the triumph of a principle that has governed the growth of copyright law to the present. If today copyright proponents take for granted that copyright law must grow like a tree and reach for the sky, it is because in the nineteenth century, politicians, and more slowly judges,[1] forgot the old injunctions that copyright laws must encourage learning. Gradually, they accepted the publishers' argument that statute must increase, but on no account restrict, the scope of copyright. The beneficiaries of laws were private interests, not the public.

The transcendental character of justifications for authors' rights swept away most resistance to the importuning of publishers. Transcendental argument has ever since silenced opposition to the expansion of copyright laws. Authors' rights, says the argument, must be taken for granted. They do not need to be adduced: they are self-justifying, or must at least be taken as justified by necessity.

The necessity lies in the negative consequences of denying rights. Any contraction will extinguish the creative spark and risks poisoning the roots of invention. Accepting the argument, legislators progressively added to the length of the copyright monopoly. They came to believe that copyright is intended to benefit authors, and in so doing they forgot about the claims of the public. Long after the lapsing of their charter, long after the Lords rejected the possibility of perpetual copyright, the ghosts of the Stationers triumphed over the enemies of monopoly.

Once viewed as a necessary evil, the copyright monopoly soon came to be regarded as a necessary concession to the needs of authors, who, in its absence,

[1] In *Stowe* v. *Thomas* (1853) 2 Am Law Reg 210, Justice Greer held in circuit court that an unauthorized German translation did not infringe Harriet Beecher Stowe's copyright in *Uncle Tom's Cabin* because translation is necessarily interpretive as well as literal. The decision reflected a continuing concern in the American judiciary to ensure that copyright legislation fulfilled the public function prescribed in the copyright clause of the Constitution.

B. Atkinson and B. Fitzgerald, *A Short History of Copyright*,
DOI 10.1007/978-3-319-02075-4_5,

were said to be at the mercy of publishers and an indifferent public. Publishers spoke out on behalf of authors, spreading the idea of the helpless creator as a device to secure extension to the term and scope of copyright. Extension to the copyright term came in increments and more slowly than they liked. But eventually they won the day, and fulminations against monopolies grew more rare in public debate.

A concomitant change, symbolic as well as material, substantially altered the distribution of land in the United Kingdom between 1760 and 1840. Parliament passed over 5,000 Acts enclosing nearly 7 million acres of open or common land, a total constituting over 20 % of land in the country.[2] Land enclosed passed into private ownership. Enclosures began probably in the fourteenth century and gathered momentum after the Tudor property revolution.

Intended to produce greater and more efficient production, land privatization also proceeded from the same motive that impelled the Industrial Revolution: to find profit by feeding capital. Physical enclosure in the eighteenth and nineteenth centuries is said to be mirrored in the enclosure, by intellectual property laws, of the 'intellectual commons', which, according to contemporary critics, became noticeable in the twentieth century, and continues in the twenty-first.[3]

5.2 Fair Use

The United States passed a new Copyright Act in 1831, and then in little more than a decade, the British parliament enacted two copyright statutes: the Dramatic Copyright Act of 1833 and the Copyright Act of 1842.[4] For the rest of the century, courts in the United Kingdom would ponder the application of the old common law doctrine of fair abridgement,[5] and in the United States, the emerging doctrine of fair use.

The fair use doctrine drew upon fair abridgement principles but it also embodied a distinctively American conception of how the rights of the copyright holder must be understood and protected. In 1841, Joseph Story, a member of the Supreme Court sitting on circuit court in Massachusetts, set out, in *Folsom* v. *Marsh*,[6] the criteria for determining the circumstances in which copying did not constitute infringement. The case involved the claim that the author of the *Life of Washington* infringed the copyright of the author of *The Writings of George Washington*, by

[2] See e.g. Brown (1991) at 62.

[3] See, e.g., Boyle (2003), pp. 33–74.

[4] The UK Parliament passed a number of copyright Acts in preceding years, including the Model and Busts Act (1798), the Copyright Act (1801), the Sculpture Copyright Act (1814) and the Copyright Act (1814) amending the Statute of Anne.

[5] Codified, in modified form, by the UK Parliament in the Copyright Act 1911.

[6] 9 F.Cas. 342 (CCD Mass. 1841) (No 4, 901).

copying from the second work 255 pages consisting of letters and other documents of Washington.

Justice Story found infringement on the basis that although the defendant copied less than 4 % of the appellant's work, the copying involved 'clear invasion of the right of property', one that harmed the value of the work from which the pages were copied. He stated that to determine whether copying could be called fair abridgement, a court must 'look to the nature and objects of the selection made, the quantity and value of the materials used, and the degree in which the use may prejudice the sale, or diminish the profits, or supersede the objects, of the original work'.

In so doing, he stated the essential elements of the fair use defence that US courts apply today, and which Congress codified in 1976.[7] Viewed by the majority of observers as the preserver of the public's liberty to use copyright material freely, and without authorization, in certain circumstances, the doctrine of fair use has also attracted criticism. A corpus of academic writing has commented severely on Story's inference that the copyright monopoly encompassed a right to restrain the copying of portions of a work.

The Copyright Act of 1831 vested in the copyright holder the right to control the 'printing, reprinting, publishing and vending' of a book, not the right inferred by Story to control reproduction of portions. According to critics, Story's judgment brought harmless uses within the rubric of infringement, expanding the scope of the copyright monopoly beyond anything envisaged by the 1831 legislators or the framers of the 1790 Act.[8]

5.3 Mercantilism

A decade separated the passing of the US Copyright Act of 1831, and its British counterpart of 1842, and both lasted into the first decade of the next century, the first Act replaced in 1909 and the second in 1911. Of the two, the most significant is perhaps the Copyright Act of 1842, which stood for the principle that copyright principally protected publishers from piracy. The Act passed after the most famous debate over copyright heard in the British parliament, a debate illuminated by a speech on the subject widely regarded as the greatest in parliamentary history.

At the time when parliament debated the copyright bill of 1841, the publishers were greatly assisted, on both sides of the Atlantic, by government trade policy. The free trade movement took hold in the United Kingdom in the nineteenth century but even when ostensibly encouraging free trade between its possessions, Britain controlled their trade policy. Publishers became expert mercantilists, and succeeded in gaining control of the production and distribution of copyright works throughout the British Empire. Colonies and dominions were compelled by imperial copyright

---

[7] United States Copyright Act 1976 17 (Copyright) USC.

[8] See, e.g., Patterson (1998).

law to buy books published in the United Kingdom from the publishers. They could not purchase the books from any other legitimate suppliers and despite this onerous limitation, their own publishers could only reproduce British books under licence.

No such limitation applied in the United States, which exploited to the hilt its policy of copyright isolation. The US refusal to recognize copyright in British works enabled American publishers to plunder the storehouse of recent English literature and sell cheap copies to the increasingly vast American public. US publishers, however, were jealous of their copyrights, and like their British counterparts pressed for the extension of legal rights.

5.4 Macaulay and Copyright Term

Before 1842, the parliamentary petitions of authors such as the poet Wordsworth popularized the idea of a creative work as a personal possession belonging by natural right to the author. Writers like Robert Southey and Charles Dickens passionately accepted the argument of natural rights and they inspired Thomas Noon Talfourd, a parliamentarian and a friend of Wordsworth, to advocate for more extensive protection of literary property. He introduced his first copyright bill in 1837 but his second bill, introduced on 29 January 1841, began again the great debate over copyright's duration.

Although he stated that justice demanded perpetual copyright, Talfourd sought a copyright term of life of the author plus 60 years. His three speeches on his first copyright bill, delivered between 1837 and 1839, traced the history of the debate over perpetual copyright, and observed the contributions and privations of authors. Talfourd's arguments attracted considerable support. The possibility that the family of Sir Walter Scott would soon lose copyright in his works may have aroused the sympathy of the House of Commons.[9]

However, the term proposed by Talfourd failed to win the final support of the majority of parliamentarians. Although some academic opinion has turned against the thesis that he played a determinative role in turning politicians against a long posthumous term, the historian and poet Thomas Babington Macaulay spoke brilliantly against long publishing monopolies.

In 1831, Macaulay made his parliamentary reputation with a brilliant speech in support of the reform bill that improved the electoral system and enlarged the franchise. Though he was at the height of his literary success, he did not share the opinions of Wordsworth and Dickens. Unlike Dickens, who spoke of the wickedness of copyright piracy, he regarded copyright as a necessary evil not a moral necessity. The legislature, he said, need only to look to the public interest, not the heavens or natural law, to determine how copyright should be constituted. The

[9] Evidence of John Henry Parker, retired publisher, before the Royal Commission on Copyrights 1875–1878, quoted in Plant (1934).

rights of the copyright holder were, he believed, subordinate to the needs of the public.

Macaulay's criticism of lengthy posthumous copyright is remembered not only for biting wit and excoriation of monopoly. He identified, implicitly, information dissemination as the true object of policy. In this way, he anticipated later economic theory explaining the purpose of copyright regulation. Macaulay placed readers' interests before those of authors or publishers. His career of copyright controversy lasted for little more than a year, from the introduction of a copyright bill in January 1841 until the appearance of its successor in March 1842. The bill passed on 1 July 1842 but only after parliamentarians considered every detail of the arguments submitted.

If Macaulay did not carry the bill or win the debate he impressed many with arguments in favour of a reduced copyright term as well the formula of life plus 7 or 42 years from publication, whichever occurred later.[10] An infrequent parliamentary speaker, he rose on 5 February 1841, after hearing Talfourd speak in support of the bill, to make the second of his two famous speeches in the Commons.[11]

Macaulay summarized the dangers of copyright in a few sentences. He considered the long posthumous term an evil rather than copyright in itself, which he thought a 'necessity' to remunerate authors, although the 'tax is an exceedingly bad one'. He accepted in principle the human expectation that property passes from one generation to the next, and considered this expectation sufficient reason to allow posthumous copyright. But, he said, reality often disappointed the expectations of heirs.

Since a posthumous term promised future profit, third parties would bid for valuable copyrights, and authors would often sell the property—the heir's expected benefit—to the highest bidder. Copyright would pass into the hands of strangers, and they would fix production and price as their monopoly rights permitted. The longer the term of monopoly, the worse for the public, which, instead of enjoying free access to literature, must, until the term lapsed, accept frequently onerous terms of supply.

Turning to the other main argument for posthumous copyright, that it provides the author with an incentive to produce for the economic benefit of descendants, Macaulay ridiculed the idea that copyright holders worked to benefit their descendants. Macaulay regarded copyright as a rational alternative to a system of patronage but he could see no justification for laws that would make copyright a commodity traded into the distant future. Copyright should exist for one reason only, to remunerate professional authors. Natural law justifications for copyright were, according to Macaulay, absurd.

---

[10] According to a witness to the Gorell Committee in 1909, Macaulay chose the period of 42 years because the debate over the second bill took place in 1842: evidence of Charles Whibley to Gorell Committee (1909)—*Appendix of Statements of Evidence Submitted to the Committee* (Cd 5051).

[11] The first of two speeches on the copyright bill.

Macaulay established for posterity a concept of public interest. He also pointed out that rights awarded for a legitimate cause—in modern terms, the protection of investment from free-riding—may be subverted. He rejected the idea of copyright as a near-sacred commodity, voicing the scepticism that informed, but did not significantly influence, copyright debates in the twentieth century.

5.5 A Different Attitude to Copyright

Macaulay's speech in 1841 against a lengthy copyright term could be interpreted as a last tolling of the bell for the idea copyright law should be subservient to public needs. The judgment of Justice Story in *Folsom* v. *Marsh*, delivered in the United States in the same year that Macaulay addressed the House of Commons, signalled the direction that copyright law development would afterwards take.

By imputing to the statutory right to print, reprint, publish and vend,[12] permission to control the reproduction of any part of a book or manuscript, Justice Story established the copyright holder as the object and beneficiary of copyright law. The holder's control over use, Story seemed to imply, is absolute, save for the limited possibilities for unauthorized use permitted by principles he outlined.

Macaulay's appeal to public benefit, prefigured in earlier statutory statements that copyright legislation is intended to encourage learning, was repeated and elaborated in public debates over copyright for over 150 years. In that period, however, Story's conception of the copyright holder's primary entitlement to control all uses of copyright material, expressed by a multitude of like-minded advocates, won the support of legislators on both sides of the Atlantic, and, assisted by the development of international law in favour of authors' and neighbouring rights, across the world.

From the middle of the nineteenth century, the demands of capital, and its modern corollary, mass production, created an acquisitive hunger from which the supporters of authors' rights were not immune. They too sought to harness the forces of capital, and control the process of production and distribution. They also sought control of the multiplication of copies by advocating for new legal categories that recognized copyright not in physical objects, like books or manuscripts, but in the abstract *works* embodied in these objects.

Thus copyright proponents shifted in the direction of recognizing distinctions identified by the German idealists, and finding statutory ways to enable copyright holders to profit from control over all forms of reproduction. By these actions, they disavowed the long Western tradition, expressed in Platonic idealism, Aristotelian ethics, Stoicism, patristic teaching and medieval scholasticism, of hostility to concentred ownership.

[12] US Copyright Act 1831, s1.

Though they spoke romantically of the author's vocation, they pressed hard for mercenary reward. They found no difficulty in upholding their claims, even while myriad nineteenth-century social dissenters identified in the expansion and concentration of proprietary rights the primary causes of exclusion and injustice.

While insisting on entitlement justified by appeal to natural rights, copyright proponents embraced the materialism of their age, and sought control and profit to the exclusion of other considerations. In this respect, they obeyed the logic of the Stationers' Company: find patrons, control, exclude. Needless to say, their attitude towards output would have confounded members of most non-Western societies, many of whom regarded literary or artistic output as the expression of tradition, or an individual's vision of reality articulated within the conventions of tradition.

Belonging to cultures that safeguarded custom and drew sustenance from ancient mores, they would not dream of permitting possessive appropriation by individuals of knowledge, artwork or writing considered to be the birthright of a people, not the endowment of a person.

References

Boyle J (2003) The second enclosure movement and the construction of the public domain. Law Contemp Probl 66:33–74

Brown R (1991) Society and economy in modern Britain 1700–1850. Routledge, London

Patterson LR (1998) Folsom v. Marsh and its Legacy. Scholarly Works, Paper 351. http://digitalcommons.law.uga.edu/fac¬_artchop/351

Plant A (1934) The economic aspects of copyright in books. Economica 1(2):167–95

Chapter 6
Property, Copyright and Copyright Internationalism

6.1 The Surge of Capitalism

The second half of the nineteenth century released in Britain and the United States an extraordinary surge of capitalist energy, as the barons of enterprise, supported by a willing middle class, sought profit in every form of production. Railways criss-crossed both countries, conquering distance and integrating economies. Steel ships powered by steam, and later internal combustion, replaced canvas-rigged sailing vessels and carried exports to expanding markets.

Chemical, electrical, petroleum and steel industries, giants born from scientific discovery, made possible miraculous infrastructure developments that changed the landscape of the industrial world. Later came the invention of the telephone and production of the motor car. Applications for patents soared as productive enterprise increased the thirst for innovation.

In Britain, the wonders of domestic growth were often identified with the acquisition of colonies, and many saw in the nation's leadership of industrial production the justification for possessing the world's greatest empire, brimming with markets and sources of supply. Americans mostly considered empire a kind of succubus, draining a nation's moral and material energies. But differences over the merits of colonial expansion were easily forgotten in capital's headlong rush to conquer the earth.[1]

In a climate of prodigious economic energy, the trend towards more invention and more production could not fail to affect the narrow world of copyright, until now defined by the accommodations of authors and publishers. Writers and

[1] Rudyard Kipling's poem 'The White Man's Burden', published in 1899, referred to US imperialism in the Philippines. The United States annexed the Philippines from Spain in 1898, after the Spanish-American War, and waged war on Filipino independence forces under Emilio Aguinaldo until he declared allegiance in 1901. Americans tended to be contemptuous of British imperialism but the majority viewed US annexation of Spanish territory in a different light. Many, however, such as Mark Twain, who initially supported war against the Spanish, opposed US adventurism. Twain helped found the American Anti-Imperialist League in 1898.

B. Atkinson and B. Fitzgerald, *A Short History of Copyright*,
DOI 10.1007/978-3-319-02075-4_6, © Springer International Publishing Switzerland 2014

composers learnt to feel aggrieved. Why should they be excluded from the fruits of material progress? As markets for books expanded worldwide, should they not reap an increasing reward? The invention, towards the end of the nineteenth century, of machines for recording sounds, and playing recordings, fuelled their sense of grievance. If an invention allowed manufacturers to profit from the use of their works, then were they not entitled to share in the profits?

By the beginning of the twentieth century, advocates of authors' rights loudly vented their bitterness. Machines for playing sound recordings, usually called phonographs,[2] were transforming society in the United States, Great Britain and Europe. Millions bought phonographs and listened to records at home or at public entertainment venues.

Popular music, and other types of recorded entertainment, changed attitudes and influenced social mores. The manufacturers of phonographs and records made fortunes from popular demand for music but they paid nothing to the lyricists or composers who created the works they recorded.

Contending in a world devoted to material gain, the proponents of authors' rights determined that principles of copyright must extend beyond the production of books, drawings and sheet music to embrace any use of copyright works that created profit. The phonographic industry used copyright material to make profit and authors asserted a right to control the use of material. In the acquisitive spirit of the age, they made clear that they intended to control the use of material by any new industry. Control would be exerted not to preserve artistic integrity but to secure a share of profits.

6.2 The Age of Property

One historian has divided the years between 1850 and 1914 into consecutive periods of unequal length, calling the first the age of capital and its successor the age of empire (see Hobsbawm 1989, 1996). Others see a half century or more in which the march of science and growth of material welfare are accompanied by a deadly rivalry of European nations arguing over possessions and resources in other continents. Rivalry ends in the dark night of the First World War and so too belief in

[2] Thomas Edison made the first phonographic recording in 1877 and patented his invention in 1878. Edison's sound recordings were made on cylinders. Emile Berliner, a German who became a US citizen, invented the gramophone disc record in 1888 and henceforward gramophones were classified as machines that played disc records. Berliner founded the US Gramophone Company in 1892 and sister companies were incorporated in Great Britain and Germany in 1897 and 1898. Disc recordings proved far more popular with the public than cylindrical records and Edison ceased manufacture of phonograph cylinders in 1929. The terms 'phonograph' and 'gramophone' were, however, often used interchangeably. In the United States, record players were more often referred to as phonographs. In copyright debates in the United Kingdom in the years leading up to the passing of the Copyright Act 1911, record players were commonly called phonographs. In the UK after the First World War, the term 'gramophone' replaced 'phonograph'.

the inevitable victory of rationalism and the curative value of twin godheads, profit and progress.

The period 1850–1914 may also be called, and more precisely, the age of property. Nations concentrated their energy on production, trade and acquisition, activities that depended on legal recognition of definable subject matter—in short, property. They made property of foreign territory as readily as, a few generations earlier, they had made property of West African captives transported across the Atlantic to work as slaves. They made property of the products of their new territories and they converted those products, and other materials, into still more items of property to be delivered to the domestic market or exported.

Acceptance of legal precepts of private property, and the individual's moral entitlement to lawfully acquire property without limitation, united the legislatures and voting populations of both Great Britain and the United States. Voters might disagree on religion, imperialism, working conditions or methods of production, but most recognized the right to private property as the guarantor of present and future progress.

Political instincts were shaped, especially in the United States, by three centuries of Calvinist theology. The Calvinism spread to America by Puritan emigrants from England taught men to disavow political absolutism and to harness earthly resources for useful purposes. For generations, gentlemen politicians felt the obligation to confirm, by private effort, their election for salvation, and they shaped the polities of two nations. The idea of an individual's freedom to determine truth encouraged belief in political equality and the urgent necessity to demonstrate personal worthiness encouraged belief in the rightness of industry.

Societies on both sides of the Atlantic came to revere material gain, even if prosperity seemed mostly to benefit a small minority of society. Ownership identified a citizen as a useful creature and long before the nineteenth century philosophers of liberty like John Locke had supplied the justification for ownership on any scale. If a person laboured, so the person deserved to own the fruits of labour, and if labour involved the expropriation (or alienation) of land, so that person deserved to possess, or own, the land.

Moral certainty about the necessary connection between property and progress inspired a seemingly irresistible drive to privatization. Individuals and nations sought to annex more land, create more possessions and produce more goods. In theory, property rights could apply to anything that could be defined. It is scarcely surprising that when new technologies promised new ways of disseminating copyright material, the authors' rights movement insisted on the author's right to annex as property modes of dissemination unrelated to the publication of books or sheet music.

However, the age of property is so-called not only because millions chose to follow a gospel of private appropriation and the pursuit of wealth. Others, thinkers and revolutionaries, resisted, with their own materialist theories, the dominant materialism of the age. They opposed the appropriation credo and created contrary intellectual movements that, in varying degrees, influenced later opponents of extensive intellectual property rights.

6.3 Opposition to Property

From the late eighteenth century, the Industrial Revolution attracted the criticism of social theorists who declared that the growth of industry resulted from exploitation. Critics refused to support an economic system that produced wealth and human misery in gross measure.[3] Beginning with the French social thinker Henri de Saint-Simon (d. 1825), a line of utopians and revolutionaries from Robert Owen in Britain (d. 1858) to the Frenchmen Charles Fourier (d. 1837) and Louis Blanc (d. 1882) identified themselves as *socialists*, or those who believed in either collective ownership of the means of production or equitable distribution of ownership.

Anarchists as diverse as Pierre-Joseph Proudhon (d. 1865) and Mikhail Bakunin (d. 1876) went further than the socialists and rejected altogether enforceable authority. Proudhon regarded property as an obstacle to free and beneficial social organization. Bakunin argued that capital and all its manifestations or products were intrinsic to political power and must be destroyed. However, during the later nineteenth century, democratic politics nullified the revolutionary potential of the different species of socialist or anarchist doctrine. Then, as now, prosperity and peace seemed to cauterize disaffection and vanquish impulses to political extremism.

One political theory—communism—asserted the consequences of property accumulation with such menacing precognition that its principles and prophecies could be neither accommodated nor disregarded by liberal society. Its founding genius, Karl Marx, published the *Communist Manifesto* and *Das Kapital* in 1848 and 1867.[4] He argued that the bourgeoisie's ownership of the means of production enabled it to generate and control capital, and reap the benefits of its use.

Ownership accrued to a minority and to survive the vast mass of population, the proletarians, were forced to sell their labour—the source of ownership according to John Locke—to the capitalist. The capitalist, the owner, took advantage of unequal bargaining power and exploited them. Private property created prosperity for the bourgeoisie and excluded the proletariat from material benefit. Marx informed his readers that the consequence of exclusion is revolution.

---

[3] The idea that material progress relied on social exploitation came to underpin critiques of colonialism, which saw the partial benefits of imperialism (the spread of education, the rule of law and so on) as the positive by-products of an enterprise motivated by the desire of colonial powers—or their citizens—to appropriate for private profit. In recent decades, proponents of the special rights of Indigenous peoples refined such critiques, arguing that appropriation of Indigenous lands by 'invader' powers resulted in a new form of society: one that substituted property relations for what Karl Marx (in the *Communist Manifesto*) called 'idyllic relations', replacing societies allegedly based on co-existence with nature with ones that demanded appropriation of resources, production and supply predicated on consumption. Exploitation is seen as the motif of such society and property the expression of this motif. Displacement—and destruction—of Indigenous peoples unable, or unwilling, to conform to the demands of invader societies is seen as the consequence of heedless application of the ideology of material progress.

[4] *Das Kapital*, vol. 1 by Marx published in 1867; vols 2 and 3 by Friedrich Engels published in 1885 and 1894.

6.4 Marx and Copyright

The Marxian critique of property relations is relevant to analysis of copyright because it contradicts the assumption of *entitlement* that buttresses conventional arguments in favour of copyright. If, as Marx suggested, the creation of private property is an act of exploitation, then, from the perspective of social equality, entitlement to copyright protection does not exist. The contrary argument asserts that production increases social welfare and that copyrights stimulate production because legal protection against imitators creates incentive to invest.

Policy-makers and politicians favoured the second position with little hesitation, but in the modern history of copyright law-making, the undertow of Marxist thought is discernible in theoretical resistance to the expansion of copyrights. Modern arguments about copyright pay little attention to the question of the law's necessity and focus instead on its scope. Conventional arguments for copyright limitations are not difficult to reconcile with Marxian reasoning.

If ownership is a device for controlling the means of production, then more limitations on ownership dilute control. It follows that restrictions on the length of copyright or the extent to which copyright holders can demand payment for use have the effect of increasing public access to material. Framed as a contest between private control and public access, the battle over copyright scope returns attention to the question of entitlement.

To what is the owner entitled, and on what basis? These are the great unanswered questions of copyright law. In the nineteenth century, dogmatism about the necessity for more copyright laws did not dispel doubts about their true value.[5]

In the twentieth century, the great period of copyright expansion, legislators considered the question of justification to be settled, though copyright proponents did not produce evidence to show that laws created productive incentive.[6] If nothing else, however, the Marxist critique of property informed some of the arguments of the minority who, in the twentieth century, argued against the progressive expansion of copyright law.

---

[5] Ethical objections to private property also entered public discourse about property rights in the nineteenth century. The utopian socialists, and anarchists such as Pierre Proudhon, attacked on moral grounds the exclusionary character of private property. In 1891, the Catholic Church published the papal encyclical *Rerum Novarum* (on the rights and duties of capital and labour), which defended private property ('when a man engages in remunerative labour, the impelling reason and motive of his work is to obtain property, and thereafter to hold it as his very own') but condemned exploitation.

[6] See Atkinson (2007), which examines copyright law-making in Australia and the United Kingdom to determine whether laws were intended to, or did, encourage production. Laws were passed to benefit and accommodate productive interests, not to create incentive to produce. All copyright industries arising in the twentieth century flourished without copyright protection. They secured protection for strategic reasons and to optimize profits.

6.5 Authors' Rights

The champions of authors' rights believed in the social consequences of ownership as sincerely as Marxist abolitionists. They insisted on the moral character of literary property, even as they spoke of exclusive rights that would grant authors monopoly control over production. And they were rewarded for their efforts. In the 1880s, various European nations came together to consider proposals for authors' rights and in 1886 signed the Berne Convention for the Protection of Literary and Artistic Works. The provisions of the Convention still underpin international copyright law and its acceptance fulfilled the hopes of many European writers, above all the great French novelist Victor Hugo.

Hugo died a year before signature of the Berne Convention, and can be called one of its spiritual authors, although he did not endorse the idea of a posthumous term. He founded the *Society of French Writers* with Honoré de Balzac in 1837 and in 1878 helped to establish the *International Literary and Artistic Association.*[7] At the Association's opening proceedings, he made an extraordinary address, little reproduced in English, which anticipated, in terms imaginative and emotional, later arguments for literary property.[8] 'Let's not forget the twofold principle,' said Hugo, 'a book, as such, belongs to the author but the ideas in the book belong – without exaggeration – to all mankind.'

As honorary president, Hugo lent his prestige to the Association's efforts to establish an international convention to protect the rights of authors and artists. His reputation helped to attract the participation of governments and the collaboration of officials and artists produced the Berne Convention.

Though he insisted that authors' rights were subordinate to public needs, and made sober legislative proposals for the protection of writers, he also insisted on their primary contribution to the life of nations. Authors are the progenitors of culture. Hugo's supporters declared that unless authors were rewarded, preferably in the coin of monopoly, culture would die.

Governments flocked to accept a self-serving credo expressed in the language of moral necessity. By the beginning of the twentieth century, the French concept of droit d'auteur, encompassing an author's moral right to extensive legal protections against piracy or any unauthorized use of material, held sway over the hearts and minds of interested legislators in Europe and the United Kingdom.

---

[7] *Association Litteraire et Artistique Internationale* (ALAI).

[8] See Atkinson and Fitzgerald (2011), pp 29–33 for English translation of Hugo's speech. Hugo said also, "If one of these two rights, that of the author or that of humanity, had to be sacrificed, it would of course be the right of the author, because we are solely concerned with the public interest, and I declare that the interest of the public must take precedence."

6.6 Normative Effect of Convention

The Convention established standards of copyright protection that, once implemented by member countries, created uniform norms across the conforming nations. An author domiciled in one conforming nation could expect another conforming jurisdiction to accord identical legal treatment to the author's work.

The normative function of the Berne Convention and acceptance of the principle of national treatment[9] have been its principal strengths, enabling Berne delegates to generate, via standards, international copyright law. New norms, or amendments to the original Convention text, were agreed periodically at amendment conferences held on an as-needs basis. Ratification required a member nation to give effect in legislation to the minimum standard specified in the amended Convention text.

In 1886, the Convention delegates agreed, in addition to the principle of national treatment, to recognise copyright in literary and artistic works, including pamphlets, dramatic works, musical compositions, drawings, paintings, works of architecture, and sculpture, geographical charts, lithographs and illustrations. Delegates accepted an exclusive translation right. From a theoretical perspective, the Convention's most important contribution perhaps lay not in the creation of minimum standards, as influential as these became, but in its introduction of the abstract category of works, and categorical definition of copyright subject matter.

A larger substantive revision (following revision in 1896) occurred in Berlin in 1908. Among other things, delegates agreed that copyright subsisted for 50 years after the death of the author. Additionally, member nations should not make legal recognition of copyright dependent on the author carrying out formal actions such as registration. Consistent with the concept of droit d'auteur, copyright subsisted upon creation of a work.

What is perhaps most important to emphasise is the Convention's establishment, from its inception, of the category of copyright 'works'. Of equal importance, it vested in authors control over the uses of works. In this way, the Convention text demanded for authors something not previously contemplated in common law countries: exclusive control over every mode of copying, adapting, translating or disseminating any original output in the 'literary, scientific and artistic domain'.

In its own language, the Convention conferred the exclusive right to control output 'whatever may be the mode or form of its expression'. Literary property embraced much more than 'books', the old, circumscribed category of copyright subject matter, and, similarly, the categories of artistic, musical and dramatic works encompassed any format in which they could be produced or transmitted.

---

[9] The national treatment principle allows a treaty signatory to award a foreign national more generous rights than those allowed its own nationals by the country of the foreign national. The reciprocity principle does not: a signatory cannot provide more generous treatment to a foreigner than that provided to its nationals by the foreigner's country.

6.7 Unifying Law

The Berne Convention generated renewed energy for authors' rights in common as well as civil law countries. In the United Kingdom, the cause never enjoyed the suasion of its counterparts in the civil law countries, especially France. However, Thomas Noon Talfourd's passion in moving the copyright bill of 1841, and the support he received from poets and writers, showed depth of feeling against perceived indifference to the poverty and hardship of writers and artists.

In the opinion of British politicians, copyright law performed the useful function of controlling the production of books and their supply throughout the empire. From the time of the first copyright statute, until Hugo's era, all shades of British political philosophy rejected sentimental claims for greater authorial privilege. Then a new class of author emerged in Russia, France and England, novelists of extraordinary psychological insight documenting with profound imaginative sympathy the agonies of Europe's social transformation.

Hugo was one such writer, whose greatest work, *Les Misérables*, portrayed the lives of the poor and wretched of Paris and surrounds, and explored especially the theme of redemption. In the 20 or more years before the signing of the Berne Convention, when he and ALAI pressed most actively for authors' rights, opinion in Britain changed. Many saw the great novelists as olympic figures divining the spirit of the age, and politicians, impressed by the prestige of Hugo's name, flocked to support his cause.

In the meantime, lawyers, and a few legislative reformers with little feeling for literature, began to follow the lead of Talfourd. The stuttering movement for copyright law reform in nineteenth-century Britain began a few years before agreement of the Berne Convention. In 1875, the British government, faced with the continuing problem of American piracy of British books, and the Canadian market's reliance on US copies, convened a royal commission to inquire into the nation's copyright law.[10]

That law, according to the Commission, was 'destitute of any sort of arrangement'. The principal copyright legislation, the 1842 Copyright Act, gave publishers control over the production and distribution of books, but otherwise obscure statute piled upon statute, each dealing with distinct subject matter and sometimes in contradictory terms.

The Commission delivered its report in 1878,[11] finding that the copyright laws of Britain were in urgent need of consolidation and improvement. The report noted that to resolve the problem of American piracy, Britain should enter into a copyright trade agreement with the United States allowing for mutual recognition of copyright. Few recommendations were unanimous. Many were contested because the commissioners disagreed on questions of trade and economics and their application to copyright law. The only economist among the commissioners, Sir Louis

[10] Royal Commission on Copyright United Kingdom 1875.

[11] United Kingdom Report of the Royal Commission on Copyright 1878 C 2036.

Mallet, formally dissented from the Commission's decision to reject the Board of Trade's submission proposing the abolition of copyright.

The majority of commissioners (including the writer Anthony Trollope) were influenced by the *Association for the Protection of the Rights of Authors* and affirmed that copyright must be a proprietary right. As well as refusing the Board of Trade's abolition proposal, they rejected a scheme for statutory royalties to remunerate authors. The 1878 Royal Commission report is important not because of its direct influence—in the absence of pressing necessity, government neglected copyright law reform for the rest of the century—but because it helped to prepare the way for the authors' rights movement.

The lobbying of the Association for the Protection of the Rights of Authors, the insistent demand for proprietary rights and the call for a uniform streamlined law implanted in the mind of British officialdom seeds of receptiveness. When the time came, government needed little coaxing to support the expansionary programme that would be adopted at Berne. If a date is needed for the beginning of political assent in Britain to the programme of the authors' rights movement, that date is 1878.

In the common law world, the infrastructure of an international copyright regime began to emerge soon after the signing of the Berne Convention in 1886. In the same year, the British parliament passed the *International Copyright Act*, which implemented obligations under the Convention and abolished registration requirements. In 1891, the US Congress passed the *International Copyright Act* (the *Chace Act*), which extended US copyright protection to foreign authors.

6.8 Independence of the United States

The United States, however, stood apart, and would not join the Berne Union until more than a century after its inception (in 1989). From the late nineteenth century, US copyright policy, like that of the United Kingdom, expressed the purposes of government departments determined, in a contentious world, to secure the best commercial conditions for the nation's publishers, authors and purveyors of recorded music. Britain accepted the rhetoric of authors' rights, willingly implementing the compulsory provisions of the Convention, and ruthlessly enforced preferential trade rules throughout its empire.

The United States chose to avoid involvement in international law that embraced an expansive vision of authors' rights (one inspired by natural law conceptions and their corollary moral rights). Accepting the prescripts of Berne would nullify the benefit of the insular copyright policy that permitted US publishers to freely copy foreign books and sell copies cheaply to the public.

The Chace Act worked increasingly to limit the effect of this policy and US policy-makers were conscious that the unflagging growth in domestic enterprise and output would eventually cause the United States to demand that foreign jurisdictions ban the piracy of exported American copyright products. Mutual protections would then be desirable.

But the need for mutuality lay some distance in the future. The primary concern for US copyright holders remained the domestic market. To encourage uniformity in geographically proximate markets—none of them (other than Canada) English-speaking—and to spread the message that copyright law is an economic instrument, a creature of statute rather than natural law, the US government entered into bilateral and multilateral trade agreements with South and Latin American countries.

In the Americas, opportunities for treaty-making independent of Berne abounded.[12] A multilateral copyright treaty agreed at Montevideo in 1889 established a South American precedent, albeit ill-starred, for mutual upholding of copyrights.[13] The United States signed copyright conventions in Mexico City (1902) and Buenos Aires (1910), the first with all the countries of Central America other than Panama and the second with most of the countries of South and Central America (although Mexico joined in 1964).

The *Buenos Aires Convention on Literary and Artistic Copyright*, purportedly abolished formalities as a requirement for the recognition of copyright and enjoined member states to recognize each others' copyrights, provided that copyright holders imprinted on works published the term 'all rights reserved'.

The United States, however, applied the proviso abolishing formalities inconsistently, continuing to enforce the registration requirements of US copyright law. But the flouting of the convention hardly mattered: it functioned principally to benefit US exporters who sent books, sheet music and, later, records to a sizeable body of consumers in the southern continent.

US practice at the beginning of the twentieth century thus mirrored its practice at the century's close. The US government energetically concluded copyright trade deals with various nations that facilitated the smooth flow of copyright goods from the United States to willing importers. At the same time, it never lost sight of its larger interest in ensuring that international copyright law did not function in ways inimical to US economic concerns.

The acute strategic awareness of US government agencies, which, for a century, had advanced US economic interests more skilfully than counterparts in countries bothered about international copyright rules, led later to the creation of the Universal Copyright Convention (1952) and the suborning of international copyright policy to the aims of the World Trade Organization (1994).

---

[12] From the late nineteenth century until 1950 South American nations agreed the following copyright conventions: *Treaty of Montevideo on Literary and Artistic Property* of 1889, Mexico City *Pan-American Convention* of 1902, Rio de *Janeiro Pan-American Convention* of 1906, Buenos Aires *Pan-American Convention* of 1910, *Caracas Agreement* of 1911 (Bolivarian Congress), *La Habana Pan-American Convention* of 1928, *Second Treaty of Montevideo* on Intellectual Property of 1939, Washington *Pan-American Convention* of 1946.

[13] *Treaty of Montevideo on Literary and Artistic Property* 1889. The treaty provided for application of the law of the complainant's country of origin (or place of first publication) and enforcement according to the law of the place of judgment. By the time of the Second World War, non-South American members included France and Spain but the treaty's influence never grew as it might have done. The country-of-origin requirement and the non-participation of the United States stymied its growth.

6.9 Imperial Copyright

As treaty-based systems of international copyright law began to develop from the end of the nineteenth century, the United Kingdom, though keenly adhering to the Berne Convention, also encouraged acceptance of uniform rules for the distribution of books and other copyright material throughout its empire. These rules gave effect to imperial copyright legislation, which itself substantially satisfied the demands of British publishers, who, long before the American Revolution, insisted that British possessions accept exclusively the supply of books published in Britain.

In the early twentieth century, few autonomous British possessions (dominions such as Australia and South Africa) cavilled at accepting the prescripts of publishers mediated by the imperial government. The empire became an insular trade zone in which British publishers controlled the distribution or supply of books, and from which these publishers could effectively exclude English language competitors—independent prospective publishers in the imperial possessions and the piratical publishers of the United States.

The imperial copyright system is chiefly of interest today for two reasons. The first is that the longevity of its governing principle[14] showed that the existence of international copyright law does not preclude the existence of legally sanctioned international restrictive trade practices governing the distribution and sale of copyright material.

The second is that it prefigured the modern association of international copyright law with international trading rules. Although the partial harmonization of copyright and trade law under the auspices of the World Trade Organization (WTO) supposedly facilitates uniform treatment in the supply and sale of copyright material,[15] critics argue that ideals of fairness and mutual benefit, supposedly integral to both imperial and WTO systems, are not obviously motivating factors in the creation of international trade rules that benefit the copyright producers of a primary trade power—in the case of imperial copyright the United Kingdom and in the case of the WTO the United States.[16]

[14] Import controls, or parallel importation restrictions, were preserved in the copyright legislation of many former British imperial possessions for most of the twentieth century. Some copyright legislation retains import control provisions even in the twenty-first century. They allow domestic copyright holders (often agents of foreign producers) to prevent competitors from undercutting them by supplying the domestic market with cheaper legitimate product obtained from foreign markets. The result is price discrimination and restrictive supply arrangements—to the detriment of domestic consumers.

[15] The WTO administers the Trade Related Aspects of Intellectual Property Rights Agreement, which establishes minimum levels of protections members must give to the intellectual property of other members. It thus prescribes a uniform system for the trade of intellectual property (IP) products. Significantly, the TRIPS Agreement also establishes standards and procedures for enforcement of IP rights and resolution of disputes over compliance and enforcement.

[16] For discussion of imperial motives in the creation of import controls in Australia and other British dominions, see Atkinson (2007). A significant body of texts, most published between 1995 and 2005, has examined US influence over the development of international trade and enforcement

6.10 Authors' Rights Curtailed

The framers of the Berne Convention sensibly provided for revision of its terms, or their supplementation, at conferences of members, who effected changes by unanimous resolution. Revision conferences ensured the vitality of the agreement for over 80 years. The last of seven conferences took place in Paris in 1971, as did the first in 1896 (usually referred to as a conference 'completing' the first Berne conference). Interim meetings were held in Berlin (1908), Berne (additional protocol in 1914), Rome (1928), Brussels (1948) and Stockholm (1967).[17]

Victor Hugo and his collaborators considered recognition of authors' rights a moral necessity but their motives were also mercenary. They wanted copyright laws to give creators the right to authorize—or refuse—the production of books, sheet music or phonograph records, and to vest in authors control over the performance of plays or music. Such rights enabled creators to bargain more effectively for reward, but they did not alter the substance of bargains struck between most copyright holders and the publishers of books and sheet music.

The balance of economic power still tilted in favour of publishers who knew that economic necessity forced most writers and composers to agree oppressive contractual terms in order to enter the market. They doubtless welcomed the increased scope of copyright enjoined by the Berne Convention. It offered new ways to profit from copyrights, and most authors were willing to assign their copyright to publishers.

But a new industry that, ironically, began to grow from roughly the time of the signing of the Berne Convention looked with increasing disfavour on a new demand—that the Convention declare that copyright extend to 'indirect appropriations' of musical works.

By the early twentieth century, the phonographic industry had grown rich by making, without consent of the copyright holder, sound recordings of performances of musical works—and selling millions of records to the owners of phonographs (or gramophones, as record players would become known).

Composers of music—the owners of copyright in the musical works 'appropriated'—received no payment from the phonographic industry for the use made of their works. In England, they registered a protest in the courts and were rebuffed.

In 1899, in *Boosey* v. *Whight*,[18] the High Court determined that perforated paper rolls fed into an Aeolian, a mechanical wind instrument resembling a piano, functioned as part of the instrument and were not sheets of music under the 1842 Copyright Act. Justice Stirling said that perforated music rolls were 'used simply as

rules for the distribution of IP goods. Two of the more influential authors are John Braithwaite and Peter Drahos (who has published a number of related works). See, for example, their study *Global Business Regulation* (2000).

[17] The text was amended in 1979, though not by conference.

[18] 1 Ch 836.

parts of the machine for the purpose of the production of musical sounds' and the Act merely granted the right of 'multiplying copies of something in the nature of a book'.[19]

In short, the framers of copyright legislation did not intend copyright to apply to mechanical processes. Had they done so, they would have declared in the 1842 Act that barrel organs or music boxes could not play musical works without the consent of composers. Outraged, the authors' rights movement attacked the judgment in *Boosey* and insisted that copyright must apply to all modes of mechanical reproduction.

6.11 The Berlin Revision Conference

In 1908, the Berne Union convened a revision conference in Berlin, altering the Convention in a number of important ways.[20] The most significant change agreed declared that authors should possess the right to authorize mechanical recording of musical works and the public performance of the embodied works. The phonographic industry responded by pressing, with furious urgency, arguments against this manifestation of authors' rights.

The industry's leaders felt aggrieved on two grounds. First, they disputed the proposition that copyright properly subsisted in products resulting from mechanical processes for capturing, or 'fixating', copyright works in material form. Second, they were concerned that one or two phonographic companies would drive the others out of business by purchasing the majority of valuable copyrights and creating a production monopoly.

By force of argument, or weight of economic power, the industry's representatives persuaded delegates at the Berlin conference to qualify the author's right to control mechanical reproduction. The amended Convention text stated that author's must control the mechanical reproduction and performance of musical works but also provided that legislatures could make grant of the mechanical right subject to 'reservations and conditions'.

The success of the phonographic industry in persuading the Berne Union to qualify its assertion of a mechanical right for authors symbolized the beginning of the transformation of copyright law into an instrument of industrial power. At the Union's 1928 Rome revision conference, the radio broadcasting industry, thanks to

---

[19] At 539.

[20] Changes included provisos that translations, adaptations, arrangements of music and other transformative reproductions of literary and artistic works were now to be protected as original works. Members were forbidden from making the grant of copyright dependent on formalities. The revision also confirmed the principle of national treatment. The Convention stipulated a 50-year posthumous term for copyright works, although members were not obliged to give effect to the proviso in domestic law. The amended text recognized also a new category of 'cinematographic work'.

the advocacy of Australian and New Zealand delegates, would secure a similar limitation. At that conference, the Union agreed to qualify the proviso asserting the author's right to authorize broadcasts of works, permitting member nations to limit in legislation the scope of the broadcast right. In time, a separate convention on so-called 'neighbouring rights' would define producers' copyright, or the copyright of the record and film producers and broadcasters.

6.12 Effect in Great Britain

In Britain, the outcome of the Berlin Conference galvanized the phonographic companies and they stridently warned two government copyright committees of the dangers of legislation that introduced a mechanical reproduction right without limitations. The warning against monopoly fell on deaf ears when presented to the Gorell Committee in 1909,[21] but in 1911 a Parliamentary Grand Committee agreed that enactment of an unqualified mechanical right could cause disaster to the phonographic industry.

The Grand Committee amended the 1911 copyright bill to permit the compulsory recording of musical works, a change that, once the bill passed into law as the Copyright Act 1911, permitted phonographic companies to continue to record musical works without permission. To compensate copyright owners for compulsory appropriations, they were required to pay a royalty of 1.5 % of the sale price of each copy of a record embodying a musical work.

British dominions, including Canada and Australia, enacted identical laws[22] and the principle that authors' rights must accommodate the business needs of producers—first the recording and film industries, later the radio and television industries, and still later the software industry—entered the consciousness of law-makers.

In the United States, Congress provided for a compulsory recording licence in the 1909 Copyright Act, accepting the argument of a congressional inquiry committee that the exercise of the musical recording right, if unfettered, would result in the creation of anti-competitive trusts.

The Berlin Conference, intended to make comprehensive the creator's right to control the process of producing copyright material, only partly achieved its object. The grand design of authors' rights so antagonized the phonographic industry that it demanded, and received, from legislatures not only the right of compulsory recording but also copyright in recordings themselves.

The Berlin Conference signalled the unleashing of producer activism. In the future, whenever political quarrels arose, the creative faction would accommodate the interests of the producer. The 1911 British Copyright Act, which implemented

[21] Report of the Committee on the Law of Copyright, Cd. 4976.

[22] Australian *Copyright Act* 1912 and Canadian *Copyright Act* 1921.

the provisos of the Berne Convention, attested to this fact, although its provisions favoured creators.

It established the new categories of works, conferring ownership on their authors, added the 50-year posthumous term and created—under the rubric of crown copyright—a new category of government copyright ownership. Dramatic works in cinematographic films now attracted copyright protection, and control over the making and performance of cinematograph films was also vested in the copyright owner. Authors gained copyright in translations of works, composers control over the mechanical adaptation of musical works.

However, most importantly, establishing a precedent of industry preferment, the compulsory licence permitted unauthorized recording of musical performances, subject to payment of a fee. Although parliament did not show itself as friendly to the public interest as the US Congress had two years earlier, legislators also codified the concept of fair dealings, or restricted permitted uses of copyright material. In the 1911 Act these consisted of copying excerpts of works for private study, research, criticism or review and newspaper summary.[23]

6.13 Authorization

The British Copyright Act of 1911 included another innovation, one of particular relevance to modern disputes over liability for copyright infringement.[24] This was the addition to the copyright holder's exclusive rights of the power to *authorize* the acts comprised in the rights.[25] Though the added power seemed redundant to some judges—since the exclusive rights could be said to comprehend a power to authorize[26]—it supported progressive prohibition of activity that induced, encouraged or facilitated infringement.

The statute thus opened the gates of copyright jurisprudence to notions of secondary liability, as pointed out by the English authority *Copinger on Copyright* (1915). This textbook observed that '[seemingly] the new Act has enlarged the protection accorded to an owner of a copyright by thus making it part of his

[23] The commentary accompanying the 1911 Act [per s. 2(1)(i)] noted that '[p]robably, the limits of fair dealing are exceeded whenever the use is such that it must naturally compete with and injure the sale of the original work'.

[24] Most relevantly, disputes over the alleged liability of internet service providers for copyright infringement by subscribers to the service.

[25] Section 1(2) of the 1911 Act. The Australian Copyright Act of 1905 (repealed in 1912) earlier introduced the concept of authorization (ss 13, 14, 34).

[26] Scrutton LJ in *Performing Right Society Ltd* v. *Ciryl Theatrical Syndicate Ltd* (1924) 1 KB 1 at 12 and McCardie J in *Performing Right Society* v. *Mitchell & Booker* (*Palais de Danse*) *Ltd* (1924) 1 KB 762 at 773.

monopoly to "authorise" any of the acts [of copyright]'.[27] Early cases interpreted the right to authorize acts comprised in the copyright to apply to circumstances in which defendants, without consent of the owner, authorized third parties to exercise one of the exclusive rights.[28]

In Australia, the highest authority eventually construed the verb 'to authorize' to mean to 'sanction, approve, countenance',[29] although authority also stated that alleged inducement must be demonstrated by related acts of third party infringement.[30] In the twentieth century, findings of secondary liability seemed to involve obvious application of tort principle to questions of copyright infringement.

In the United States, beginning with the judgment of Holmes J in *Kalem Co.* v. *Harper Bros* (1911),[31] the doctrine of 'contributory infringement' proscribed conduct by a defendant that directly (as in *Kalem*) or indirectly procured infringement.[32] In 1976, the US Copyright Act formally recognized the owner's right to 'do' *and* 'authorize' the acts comprised in copyright.[33] Judicial interpretation continued the application of tortious principles enunciated in contributory infringement doctrine.

The development and application in copyright law of secondary liability principles thus proceeded in unremarkable fashion for most of the twentieth century, until technology made possible intermediary contribution to mass infringement. Suddenly, the concept of authorization assumed unforeseen significance. Litigation in the 1980s over the secondary liability of the manufacturer of video recorders resulted in further refinement of the contributory infringement doctrine,[34] and in the twenty-first century, courts continue to wrestle with questions of liability concerning internet service providers and the suppliers of file-sharing technology.[35]

---

[27] Copinger (1915), at 115.

[28] *Transatlantic Film Co. Ltd* v. *Albion Cinema Supplies Co.* (1917–1923) Macg. CC 118; *Finn* v. *Pugliese* (1918) 18 SR NSW 530; *Evans* v. *E. Hulton and Co. Ltd* (1924) WN 130; *Falcon* v. *Famous Players Film Co.* (1926) 2 KB 474.

[29] *University of New South Wales* v. *Moorhouse* (1975) 133 CLR 1.

[30] *Re WEA International Inc. and WEA Music Pty Ltd* v. *Hanimex Corporation Ltd* [1978] FCA 379 (1987). In this Australian Federal Court case, Gummow J provided a learned exposition of the development of authorization principles in copyright law.

[31] *Kalem Co.* v. *Harper Bros* (1911) 222 US 55 per Holmes J at 63: 'If the defendant did not contribute to the infringement, it is impossible to do so except by taking part in the final act. It is liable on principles recognized in every part of the law.'

[32] *Gershwin Publishing Corp.* v. *Columbia Artists Management Inc.* (1971) 443 F 2d 1159 at 1162, the Court of Appeals for the Second Circuit.

[33] Section 106.

[34] *Sony Corporation of America* v. *Universal City Studios* (1984) 464 US 417.

[35] For file-sharing technology cases, see, for example, *A&M Records, Inc. v. Napster, Inc.* 239 F 3d 1004 (9th Cir. 2001); *MGM Studios, Inc. v. Grokster Ltd.* 125 S. Ct. 2764 (2005); in Australia, *Universal Music Australia Pty Ltd* v. *Sharman License Holdings Ltd.* [2005] FCA 1242.

References

Atkinson B (2007) The true history of copyright: the Australian experience 1905–2005. Sydney University Press, Sydney

Atkinson B, Fitzgerald B (eds) (2011) The library of copyright essays, vol 1–3. Ashgate, Farnham

Copinger WA (1915) The law of copyright in works of literature, art, architecture, photography, music and drama: including chapters on mechanical contrivances, 5th edn. J.M. Easton, London

Hobsbawm E (1989) The age of empire: 1875–1914. Vintage, New York

Hobsbawm E (1996) The age of capital: 1848–1875. Vintage, New York

Chapter 7
Statutory Developments and Recognition of Industries

7.1 US Copyright Politics in the Early Twentieth Century

In 1909, Congress passed a new Copyright Act that would regulate copyright affairs in the United States for 67 years, more than two-thirds of the twentieth century. The outlook of congressmen differed in a fundamental way from that of their successors who passed a new Act in 1976. Though aware of their nation's unique creative and productive capacities, they did not think, as future politicians would, of the United States as the world's primary power, responsible for overseeing the growth of peace and prosperity throughout the globe.

Instead, they accepted that the Monroe Doctrine[1] correctly identified the Americas as the nation's external locus of political influence and, more broadly, the western hemisphere (excluding Western Europe and Africa). The copyright treaties agreed in Mexico City and Buenos Aires reflected this understanding. They also revealed a provincial attitude to the need for copyright protection outside US borders, an attitude shaped by the country's insularity as a producer, and consumer, of copyright products.

In 1909, the United States was not yet the world's greatest publisher, film producer, broadcaster or developer of software products. Before the US entertainment industries created a worldwide hegemony of American culture from the 1930s onwards, politicians felt little need to press for international rules designed to help the trade prospects of copyright industries. The congressmen of 1909 thus enjoyed

[1] Augmented by President Theodore Roosevelt's 'Corollary' of 1904, which he announced in the annual presidential address to Congress. Roosevelt declared that 'flagrant cases of wrongdoing' by neighbouring states might force the US 'however reluctantly' to 'the exercise of an international police power'. The intent of the declaration was to reserve for the US the right to intervene in the economic affairs of Central American and Caribbean countries to prevent debt default.

B. Atkinson and B. Fitzgerald, *A Short History of Copyright*,
DOI 10.1007/978-3-319-02075-4_7,

freedom that their successors, beholden to the wishes of the behemoths of the publishing, entertainment and software industries, did not.[2]

Soon, the gigantic creative impulse that made the United States the most productive and inventive country on earth spawned Hollywood and the radio industry. They sent to Washington a new type of political savant, lobbyists who demanded protections to ensure that these exemplars of enterprise were not forced to default on their obligation to entertain the nation. Later, the industries contributed to politicians' election funds. The 1909 congressmen had seen only the prototypes of super-effective lobbyists, though these were forceful enough—representatives of the phonographic industry and their publisher rivals declaimed furiously in Washington against the other's cause.[3]

Unlike future lobbyists, who argued for private benefit, the record industry delegates could present their case as one motivated by considerations of public welfare. If Congress were to listen to arguments for creators to enjoy unfettered power to control recording of their works, then one or two producers would persuade creators to assign their rights, gobble up all musical copyrights and charge extortionate prices for records. As surely as monopoly production would drive the majority of record companies from the market, the public would suffer from the imposts of the monopolists.

Thus in 1909, congressmen could do what few of their later counterparts, mindful of conciliating donors of election funds, considered possible and separate public from private interest. Lobbyists would come to identify the private interest of industries with the national interest, thus circumventing altogether considerations of public welfare, but in 1909 Congress could look with relatively clear-eyed regard at how proposals for copyright law reform would give effect to, or detract from, the purpose of the constitutional copyright clause, and the policy of the first amendment.

Even so, the 1909 Act emerged from the maelstrom of politics, not the meditations of a Delphic colloquium. Politicians allowed, more or less, the forerunners of lobbyists to hammer out compromise legislative proposals that could be translated into the articles of a bill. The copyright bill grew from a meeting, organized by the Librarian of Congress, of parties petitioning for reform. A year later, when joint sittings of the House and Senate patent committees

---

[2] Litman (2006) at 280 comments that the 'process Congress has relied on for copyright revision . . . has shaped the law in disturbing ways'. The 1909 Copyright Act resulted from 'a scheme for statutory drafting that featured meetings and negotiations among representatives of industries with interests in copyright'. Their prerogatives, she implies, determined statutory outcomes.

[3] A *New York Times* article of 11 December 1906 ('Mark Twain, Lobbyist'), refers to Mark Twain lobbying in Congress over the 1906 copyright bill. The Speaker Joe Cannon provided his rooms to Twain, who, according to the *Times* saw nearly half the members of the House over more than 5 hours—to no avail. Twain 'discovered that not even his influence and popularity were great enough to save the musicians and artists; that they were doomed anyhow, and that the authors were likely to fall with them unless the bill were split' (p. 69).

reviewed the bill, the motion picture, piano roll and phonographic industries, excluded from the 1905 meeting, protested vociferously.

The bill conferred on copyright holders exclusive control over the mechanical reproduction of musical works. If passed, it would allow music publishers to destroy, or more likely control, the newer industries. Members of both houses varied wildly in their views on how to judge the mechanical reproduction provisions. Committee factions submitted four legislative proposals. Joint hearings in 1908 failed to resolve the impasse, and finally a conference of publishers and mechanical reproduction industries, ratified by house and senate committees, offered a solution: the compulsory sound recording licence. A bill introduced in February 1909 contained the compulsory licence.

7.2 The Public Interest

Like the British Copyright Act of 1911, and similar enactments in other parts of the English-speaking world, the US Copyright Act of 1909 recognized the author's exclusive right to control uses of copyright material, including the recording and public performance for profit of musical works. Like the British legislation, the US statute recognized, alongside the economic interest of creators, the commercial interest of the piano roll and phonographic industry, establishing a compulsory recording licence. But unlike its counterparts in the common law jurisdictions, the US Act unmistakably recognized a third interest, that of the public.

The constitutional framers evidently saw reason for statutory recognition of the public interest in access to copyright information, declaring that copyright law should 'promote the progress' of science and arts. Progress in these fields is self-evidently a benefit to the public, but if some equivocated over the purpose of the copyright clause, they could not doubt the intent of the first amendment. Free speech and a free press could be described, metaphorically, as torches shining light in darkness—any regulation that might extinguish them could only be seen to frustrate the constitution and, more broadly, harm the public.

The House report on the copyright bill that passed into law as the 1909 Copyright Act) noted that copyright regulation is not intended 'primarily for the benefit of the author'; rather, the law was designed 'primarily for the benefit of the public'. Law-makers needed to consider 'two questions'. The first asked, 'how much will the legislation stimulate the producer and so benefit the public', and the second, 'how much will the monopoly granted be detrimental to the public?'.

As would be the case in the United Kingdom 2 years later, legislators focused their attention on the effect of expanding copyright to include control over sound recording (or 'mechanical appropriation' of musical works). In the United States, as in Britain, legal precedent favoured the recording industry's argument that copyright in a musical work protected against unauthorized reproduction in kind, not transformative use. The principal case on the subject of mechanical reproduction occurred 1 year before the passage of the 1909 Act and involved not phonograph records but piano rolls.[4]

7.3 Compulsory Licence

Although by 1908 phonographs were rapidly superseding piano players—or 'pianolas'[5]—in the public's affection, the pianola industry continued to enjoy huge commercial success selling piano players to the American public. Piano rolls operating in pianolas took the place of the pianist playing a melody, and the publishers of sheet music regarded the pianola industry as a deadly threat to sales.

In *White-Smith Music Publishing Company v. Apollo Company*,[6] the Supreme Court decided that music rolls did not reproduce a pair of popular musical scores, even though the notations on the rolls guided a pianola's automatic production of the melodies. The Court's reasoning suggested that for the purposes of the copyright legislation, a reproduction must visibly replicate, or strongly approximate, the original. Functional perforations on rolls could not be seen as facsimiles of sheet musical scores.[7]

Defeated in the courts and uncertain about the willingness of Congress to recognize their lordship of copyright, the music publishers parlayed again with the manufacturers. The recording industry itself felt uncertain about the ultimate voting intentions of politicians and so the two sides came together determined to reach a compromise that would find favour with the legislators. The solution proposed fitted comfortably with the wishes of a legislature determined to protect public access to the cornucopia of cheaply available popular music.

---

[4] Previously, Judge Colt in the first circuit federal court of appeals found that perforated piano rolls playing music in a 'machine' (a pianola) did not literally reproduce the musical score (*Kennedy* v. *McTammany* 33 F 584 CCD Mass 1888). 'Peforated strips of paper ... are a mechanical invention made for the sole purpose of performing tunes mechanically upon a musical instrument.' In the DC circuit, Justice Shepard found that a phonographic sound recording did not constitute reproduction within the meaning of the legislation (*Stern* v. *Rosey* 17 AppDC 562 CADC 1901). 'Conveying no meaning then to the eye ... and wholly incapable of use save in and as part of a machine ... these prepared wax cylinders can neither substitute the copyrighted sheets of music nor serve any purpose which is within their scope.' Both judgments were consistent with the logic in *Stowe* v. *Thomas* 23 F Cas 201 (CCED Pa 1853), which stated that the right to print and reprint did not apply to translations.

[5] From 1898, the Aeolian Company manufactured the 'pianola', invented by Edwin Scott Votey in 1895. Although the Aeolian Company held the name trademark, the piano players of competitors were soon referred to by most of the public as 'pianolas'.

[6] 209 US 1 (1908).

[7] The judgment is interesting also for the special concurrence of Justice Oliver Wendell Holmes, who assented equivocally to the lead judgment of Justice William Day. Holmes obliquely disavowed the literalism underlying the Court's judgment. He referred, as he did in *Kalem Co.* v. *Harper Bros* 222 US 55 (1911), to the 'essence' of the copyright. The idea of protecting this 'essence' can be seen in his terse judgment in *Herbert* v. *Shanley* 242 US 591 (1917).

To prevent the formation of music trusts, or record production controlled by just one or two record companies, Congress agreed to create a compulsory licence for sound recordings. By this measure, legislators answered, or so they thought, the two questions posed in the House report. A compulsory licence, in theory, encouraged competition among record companies to record performances of a multitude of works, thus providing the public with a wide selection of records to purchase at lower prices. Copyright holders received guaranteed compensation of two cents for each sound recording made.

7.3.1 Attitude of Legislators

Legislators also amended the copyright bill to restrict the application of the author's copyright in the public performance of music to performances 'for profit'. This addendum implied an attitude to copyright's scope not shared by courts. As applied by judges since *Folsom v. Marsh*, the fair use doctrine occluded the possibility of unauthorized use of copyright material outside the range of uses narrowly ratified by the judiciary or ultimately reserved by statute. In the 60 years that followed the passage of the 1909 Act, the prevailing attitude of Congress would come to match that of the judiciary. The 1976 Copyright Act contained no trace of the 'non-profit' proviso.

In 1909, however, law-makers calculated the public interest with unparalleled directness, and in language nearly unimaginable to their modern counterparts in any country. The sound and fury of the publishers and incipient sound recording industry expressed intimations of the copyright industries' coming sovereignty on Capitol Hill.

Considerations other than those concerning the economic security of competing industries animated the thoughts of politicians. They were able to consider, with some detachment, the effect of copyrights on public and private interests.[8] The boundless productive energy that created the United States a nation friendly to the claims of property also inspired a powerful urge to undo oppression of the public by private interests.

By the end of the nineteenth century, business agglomerations controlled the US economy, and Congress passed the 1909 Act in the middle of the great era of trust-busting initiated by President Roosevelt (president 1901–1909) and continued by President Taft (1909–1913).[9] While in the United Kingdom, centuries of vested

[8] For a thorough short account of the politics and lobbying that resulted in the 1909 Act, see Litman (2006).

[9] In 1898 President McKinley appointed an Industrial Commission to investigate price-fixing in railroad construction, industrial monopoly and the effect of immigration on labour markets. President Roosevelt implemented its recommendations (made in a 1902 report to the president and Congress) dissolving 44 trusts during his two terms (1901–1909). His successor, President Taft, dissolved 90 trusts in 4 years. The Sherman Antitrust Act of 1890 established a legislative

property interest ensured that coteries of owners obtained from parliament inordinate economic privileges, in the United States—which could look back on little more than a century of private wealth creation—politicians examined sceptically claims for private preferment.

In 1909, legislators happily extended the reach of copyright, but decided that musical performance, which focused the attentions of musical composers, a burgeoning recording industry and, most importantly, supply of millions of consumers of piano rolls, pianolas, phonographs and phonographic records must be regulated in the public interest. In other words, whatever the claims of private interests, the fact of mass public consumption of recorded music demanded that such music must be distributed to the market as efficiently as possible—for the benefit of consumers.

The corollary of this working premise—which resulted in the compulsory licence—was delimitation of musical copyright to protect private non-pecuniary use of a record. This particular delimitation, modest and reasonable, protecting the public from intrusion and the oppressive use of legal rights by copyright owners, established a precedent that was not followed. As modest as it was, it could not have won favour with later legislators, who, encouraged by the industries' rhetoric of entitlement, came to regard positive limitations on proprietary rights as unnatural.

7.4 A Future of Big Industries and Private Preferment

In 1909, the ideology of property already encouraged receptiveness to the extension of copyrights. The copyright legislation of that year, however, tried to satisfy the expectations of private interests seeking profit and the public seeking liberal access to sources of entertainment and information.

Legislative accommodations created temporary equilibrium: the so-called balance in copyright regulation between private and public interests would soon shift firmly in favour of the former. The light illuminating US copyright policy, expressed in the public-minded sentiments of the 1909 House report, soon vanished, like the golden glow of a dying summer's day.

The 1909 US Copyright Act, like the British imperial Copyright Act of 1911, pointed, though indistinctly, to a future of copyright law and policy outside the comprehension of the politicians who enacted the legislation. They saw themselves as partisans for the rights of creators and guardians of the public interest. They considered that by providing for a broad range of exclusive rights they guaranteed economic justice for authors. The compulsory recording licence protected investment and guaranteed competition, for the benefit of the public.

---

basis for so-called 'trust-busting'. The Sherman Act regulated monopolistic price-fixing by industrial trusts—that is, cabals of industrial producers—and supplied the basis for the growth of competition law.

The agitators for legislation aroused a giant, the phonographic industry, and once stirred, it refused to retreat, demanding legal preferment equal to that granted the creative faction. On both sides of the Atlantic, politicians perceived the conflict between authors' rights proponents, including publishers, and the phonographic industry as the main obstacle to equitable copyright legislation. They failed to see that that competition would soon be over and that in the process of apportioning legal rights, they ought not defer recognition of public entitlement.

Inevitably, the recording industry would come to dominate publishing houses and control the copyrights of creators, just as the literary publishing industry controlled, by contract or copyright assignment, the output and returns of writers. In the legislative sphere, politicians unwittingly assisted the encroachment of private upon public. At the end of the first decade of the twentieth century, copyright law-makers tried to reconcile the demands of authors and the recording industry. Within a few decades, a new giant, the radio broadcasting industry, would war with the recording industry, and after the warring industries made peace, broadcasters would demand the protections of copyright.

By the middle of the twentieth century, copyright law regulated the activities of the giant copyright industries, and the assumptions of law-makers were coloured by the demands of those industries. The few creators who could negotiate contracts that rewarded them as much as the producers disseminating their works benefitted wondrously from the new copyright regime. Most struggled on as impecuniously as their nineteenth-century predecessors. Authors' rights, expressed in the exclusive rights and the categories of copyright, created the skeleton of the new copyright regime, but as the twentieth century progressed, the needs or wishes of creators became subsidiary to those of the industries on which they depended.

Reference

Litman J (2006) Digital copyright. Prometheus, Amherst

Chapter 8
1920–1940: Performing Right and Radio Broadcasting

8.1 The 1920s and Radio Broadcasting

Outbreak of war in Europe in 1914 drove thoughts of copyright regulation from the minds of those who had participated in the law reform agitations of the preceding decade. The horrors of the war years, however, hastened the development of copyright law as an instrument regulating the supply and consumption of mass entertainment. The war stimulated the growth of radio communication,[1] and when the wireless burst upon the world in the 1920s, societies tormented by 4 years of catastrophe turned to radio entertainment with unrestrained enthusiasm.

The age of jazz and flappers was also the age of amateurs, with thousands of 'radio hams' assembling crystal wireless sets to listen to radio broadcasts. Broadcasting stations proliferated. In 1920, a Pittsburgh radio station broadcast the results of the US presidential elections and by 1921, 32 licensed radio stations were broadcasting across the United States. In 1922, a New York station broadcast the first radio advertisements and by the end of the year 571 stations, sharing two wavelengths, were broadcasting to the nation.

Elsewhere, radio broadcasting grew in different ways. In the United Kingdom, private broadcasting gave way to government monopoly and in Australia, a 'mixed' system created a national public broadcaster alongside numerous licensed commercial stations. Music constituted the heart of radio broadcasting. By the end of the 1920s, the British Broadcasting Corporation and the National Broadcasting Company of America were devoting two-thirds of airtime to the playing of music. Radio

[1] Guglielmo Marconi patented the wireless telegraphy process in 1896. Wireless telegraphy transmitted Morse code over the airwaves. During the First World War, European and US innovators developed two-way 'radio telephony' delivered by vacuum tube. The US Marconi company pioneered multi-point communication and after the end of the War, the Marconi Company in Britain and the United States led the growth of mass radio communication via 'wireless' transmitters.

B. Atkinson and B. Fitzgerald, *A Short History of Copyright*,

DOI 10.1007/978-3-319-02075-4_8,

broadcasting facilitated and popularized changes in musical taste, creating cultures of popular music.

Radio thus delivered to the phonographic—or as it was now known, gramophone—industry a receptive national audience for music recordings, multiplying record sales. Radio listeners heard records performed or 'played' on air, and many rushed out to buy the latest 'hit'. For the record industry, the benefit of radio broadcasting could be measured in increased sales and burgeoning demand for new kinds of music. Already by the outbreak of the war in 1914, English-speaking countries, and many in Europe, could be called 'gramophone societies'.

In 1913, one-third of British households owned gramophones and in the following year, even with war convulsing the continent, the Gramophone Company sold four million records. The advent of radio accelerated the development of something unknown to the nineteenth century, the mass audience, a nation of consumers hungry for entertainment, principally in the form of musical performances.

The creation of the mass audience and the explosive growth of record and radio industries were inseparable developments, listeners stimulating and consuming the output of entertainment impresarios, writers and musicians. In the 1920s, copyright law changed from a limited form of regulation, principally benefitting publishers, to one of ever-increasing importance to the recording industry and of urgent interest to the radio industry, which saw the law's potential to cause it harm or confer great benefit.

8.2 Collecting for Playing Music

Radio broadcasting proved more far-reaching in effect than probably any other technology in the history of copyright law-making. It caused music publishers and record companies to seek (and obtain) windfall profits by taxing the public performance of music. And, following bruising wars over claims for copyright payments, it hardened the resolve of the record companies, radio broadcasters and film-makers, to emulate the legislative success of the authors' rights movement. These industries now determined to secure optimal copyright protections to secure optimal revenues from the production and dissemination of copyright material.

The battles over the public performance right were precipitated by the activities of a new type of organization, the copyright collecting society, dedicated to collecting fees for the public performance of musical works. The first collecting society, the French society of authors, composers and music publishers, began in 1851 to collect fees for the performance of musical works in cafés. In the twentieth century, as public performances of music grew to include the playing of phonographs or gramophones in public places, new societies were formed in different countries.

In 1914, music publishers in Britain and the United States formed the *Performing Right Society* and *the American Society of Composers, Authors and Publishers*. Both societies responded directly to the boom in recorded music. By the device of so-called 'collective administration'—the administration by the society of rights assigned by music copyright holders for the purpose of collecting and distributing public performance fees—they hoped to levy fees for the playing of recorded music by entertainment or leisure venues.

Fees collected would deliver, or so they thought, a financial bonanza to music publishers, which owned a large proportion of copyrights. The return to composers who retained copyright—which they usually assigned for the purpose of collective administration—was more uncertain, since fees paid for the performance of individual works were often meagre and the distribution practices of the societies often criticized as organized for the direct benefit only of the publishers.[2]

The overwhelming importance of the public performance right in copyright affairs in the years between the two world wars testifies to the way that technologies for disseminating copyright works—rather than authors' rights discourse—now shaped law-making. But for the invention of sound recording and radio broadcasting, the performing right would likely have counted as a forgotten copyright.

In the nineteenth century, the performing right enabled playwrights and musicians (or more likely theatre owners and publishers) to claim payment for the public performance of works on a stage or in concert hall. Logically, the performing right could not be reconciled with the concept of literary property, which consisted of reproductive and distributive rights. Legislators intended it as a purely pecuniary right, added to copyright legislation as an expedient to allow remuneration to two classes of creator with whom copyright law did not principally concern itself.

In the twentieth century, technological innovation changed everything. The public performance right enabled the owners of film and music copyrights to claim payment for performances to mass audiences, the aggregate of cinema goers, or patrons of entertainment venues, or listeners to radio broadcasts of sound recordings. Courts rapidly confirmed in a series of test cases that the holders of musical copyrights were entitled to enforce the right or, more specifically, charge fees to those who played music for commercial purposes.

8.3 Herbert v. Shanley

In the United States, the Supreme Court took the broadest view of commercial purpose, interpreting the 'for profit' proviso in a way that ensured that the copyright holder could expect remuneration for musical performances, even though

---

[2] Performing right collecting societies' constitutions usually require that they allocate at least 50 % of revenue collected to artists. However, since societies are usually reluctant to disclose details of income distributions, it is difficult to determine the extent to which the majority of artists are remunerated. Critics remain suspicious that collecting societies collect for big commercial interests—publishers and successful artists—and neglect smaller artists, because administering diffuse rights is time-consuming and sometimes difficult.

customers or audiences paid no fee for performances. In the leading case, *Herbert v. Shanley & Co*,[3] Justice Holmes delivered a brief Supreme Court judgment stating the liability of a pair of restaurants to pay copyright fees for their orchestras' public performances of musical works. Though patrons of the restaurants paid for food, rather than the playing of music, the price paid for the food also procured the music.

This proposition seems obvious enough, but Holmes's reasoning strikes a note of prevarication sometimes evident when the scope of a copyright is enlarged in the owner's favour.[4] He wrote that if liability depended on the restaurants charging directly for performances, '[p]erformances not different in kind from those of the defendants could be given that might compete with and even destroy the success of the monopoly the law intends the plaintiffs to have'.

The purpose of this monopoly, seemingly, was to remunerate copyright holders for public performances of music that in any way, direct or indirect, contributed to the profits of an economic activity. In the last line of his judgment, Holmes said: '[w]hether it [the musical performance] pays or not the purpose of employing it is profit and that is enough'.

While it is true that legislators designed the performing right in the nineteenth century to enable composers and dramatists to obtain revenue from concerts and plays of their works—whereas the policy of literary copyright lay in piracy deterrence—Holmes reasoned speciously. The 'for profit' proviso contemplated, consistent with the traditional policy of the performing right, that infringing performance involved performances for which the audience paid—in other words performance procured by payment of performance fees.[5]

[3] 242 US 591 (1917).

[4] For a description of Holmes's attitudes to the scope and application of copyright law, see Vaidhyanathan (2001). He suggests that Holmes purposely tried to extend the copyright owner's control to any use, 'if'—as Holmes stated in *Bleistein* v. *Donaldson Lithograph Co.* (1903) USC—'use means to increase trade and help make money'.

[5] The crucial part of Holmes's reasoning is expressed in the assertion that unauthorized performance might, 'compete with, and even destroy the success of the monopoly the law intended the plaintiffs to have'. The threat of putative economic competition necessarily implies the existence, or creation, of a market, but Holmes paid no attention to defining that market or, indeed, the meaning of a market. Conventionally defined, a market is the sum of transactions between sellers and buyers of definable goods and services. In *Herbert*, the economic transactions in question involved the sale and purchase of food in a restaurant. The diner did not negotiate or pay a defined price for the supply of orchestral services. The orchestra provided services 'for profit' *to the restaurateur*. Privity existed between restaurateur and orchestra, not diner and orchestra. Properly speaking, if 'for profit' fees were to be extracted from the restaurateur, the appropriate source from which they should be calculated would be the fees paid to the orchestra rather than the total amounts paid by diners. Additionally, Holmes's allusion to copyright as a monopoly intended to confer benefit ('success') suggested legislative intent that copyright secure remuneration in all circumstances. Holmes is thus the author, or popularizer, of copyright's remuneration fallacy. The legislative justification for the copyright monopoly is not reward but protection against free-riding in order to maintain the incentive to produce. The public performance right did not originate as a copyright but even viewed purely as a remuneration right, it could not be said historically to

Had the legislature intended otherwise, it would have dispensed with the proviso and provided that 'not for profit' performances were not remunerable. If the term 'for profit' referred, as Holmes reasoned, to performances occurring in the course of any economic activity directed to profit, the proviso became redundant. If any economic activity involving public performance gave rise to an obligation to pay performance fees to the copyright holder, then only public performances that were explicitly amateur could be considered unremunerable.[6]

Holmes thus avowed in the United States the principle of remuneration-for-use. What perturbed him was that unauthorized performance conferred an economic benefit on the restaurateurs and none on the copyright holders. That the profits he attributed to the playing of music could not be quantified did not seem to concern him. On his judgment hangs the whole of the subsequent history of judicial and legislative attitudes to copyright fees collecting in the United States. The pay-for-use principle has come to underpin economic transactions between the suppliers and consumers (or users) of copyright material.

Its logic is this: if copyright material is used incidental to, or as part of, any economic activity, the copyright owner is entitled to receive a portion of revenue generated by the activity. This principle might be called the remuneration fallacy, since the theoretical rationale for intellectual property rights must always be protection against piracy for so long as is necessary to guarantee productive incentive[7]—not the guarantee of remuneration for use. Application of the pay-for-use principle has resulted in the complex, and economically inefficient, taxation practices of collecting societies and copyright corporations. Subject to narrow limitations, they extract fees for most uses of copyright material, even though many uses occur in markets in which the copyright owners do not participate, and which neither undermine, nor, in Holmes's words, 'destroy' the copyright owners' markets.

By 1940, after bitter commercial wrangling, government and business alike accepted that copyright legislation directly facilitated the transfer of income from users of copyright material to owners of that material. In other words, the law regulated, to the convenience of copyright owners, extensive taxation of copyright use. In coming years, other categories of copyright owner emulated the model of copyright taxation created by collecting societies. By the end of the twentieth century, owners licensed, and claimed remuneration for, nearly every conceivable use of material.

comprehend the idea of taxing receipts from payments for the supply of services which, nominally at least, were unconnected with the public performance of music.

[6] See also *Jerome H. Remick & Co.* v. *American Automobile Accessories Co.* 5 F 2d 411 (6th Cir. 1925) and *M. Witmark & Sons* v. *L. Bamberger & Co.* 291 F 776 (D.N.J 1923).

[7] The exclusive rights permit the copyright holder to bargain for reward—they do not entitle the copyright owner to remuneration.

8.4 Fees Controversy

As radio listening spread rapidly through national populations in the 1920s, the Performing Right Society (PRS) in the UK began levying public performance fees on the BBC.[8] Since the broadcaster played so much music over the airwaves, revenues, already swelled by collections from entertainment venues, grew larger. But as collections grew, so too did the unhappiness of those paying levies. In 1929, the government introduced the *Musical Copyright Bill*, which introduced compulsory licensing of the performing right and established a fixed maximum fee payable to the copyright owner.

The House of Commons Select Committee that examined the bill, under considerable pressure from the PRS, criticized the compulsory elements of the legislation and instead recommended that it provide that disputes over fees could automatically be referred to 'arbitration or some other tribunal'. The Committee stated that the PRS was a 'super monopoly' controlling over 90 % of performing right copyrights. But it accepted that the PRS's undertakings were sufficient to answer the complaints of copyright users.[9]

The government, however, dropped the bill, responding not only to continued duress by the PRS but also to its own departments, which nervously argued that any form of restriction on the exercise of the performing right could breach treaty obligations under the Berne Convention. The power of authors' rights thus expressed itself in a way useful to the commercial purpose of music publishers.

In Australia, where the PRS instigated the incorporation, in 1925, of the *Australasian Performing Right Association* (APRA), the fight over enforcement of the public performance right proved more bitter still than in the United Kingdom. In the interwar period, Australia could fairly be called the home of the world's most diverse and innovative radio industry, and, judged by per capita ownership of radio sets, the most enthusiastic nation of radio listeners. Complaints over APRA's right to collect on behalf of undeclared copyright holders and the size of, and increases to, fees levied spilled into public consciousness. APRA became a reviled corporation.

In 1932, the government established terms of reference for the Royal Commission on the Performing Right, and the commission reported in 1933, recommending the establishment of a tribunal to arbitrate disputes over fees and collection practices.[10] But the Australian government, like its British counterpart, chose to

---

[8] The British Broadcasting Company, later the British Broadcasting Corporation.

[9] Music users said the PRS did not publish lists of works it claimed to control and made arbitrary increases in licence fees.

[10] The Royal Commission disagreed with the representations of the British Board of Trade and Foreign Office to the House of Commons Copyright Committee concerning treaty obligations. In 1928, thanks largely to the intransigence of the Australian and New Zealand representatives at the Berne Union's Rome revision conference, delegates agreed that the members could impose conditions on the copyright holder's exercise of the broadcasting right. As a result, the amended Berne Convention vested in the owner of works control over the broadcasting of those works but

ignore expert findings. Its inaction attested to the economic and political power of APRA, which could not only point to its legal right to collect fees for the playing of music on radio, but also aggressively cast doubt on the legislature's power to compel the arbitration of copyright disputes.

In Canada, government acted much more assertively. Parliament amended the *Canadian Copyright Act* in 1931 to require performing right societies to file with the copyright office lists of all works to which a society claimed title, and a statement of all licence fees imposed from time to time. Fees could not be levied or collected for works not included in the lists. The relevant government minister could revise or prescribe licence fees, if satisfied that a collecting society withheld the grant of a licence, collected excessive fees or otherwise acted in a manner harmful to the public interest.

8.5 Copyright Law as Guarantee of Revenues

Disputes over performing right fees were arguments about the size of mandatory revenue transfers from one set of economic actors to another. In total, the amounts transferred dwarfed the revenues of nineteenth-century publishers reliant on income from sales of books and sheet music.

Copyright law had stepped beyond the compass of sales to become a device for enabling publishers to charge public performance fees for the broadcasting of music. Fees, usually calculated as the percentage of advertising revenues, which themselves were determined by reference to the size of a broadcaster's audience, enriched some publishers and some artists.

After 1950, fees were levied for television performances, their quantum partly determined by calculation of size of audience. By the end of the twentieth century, collecting societies were charging governments, universities and schools for the privilege of photocopying materials. In short, copyright legislation guaranteed, in a convenient and predictable way, income delivery to various categories of copyright holder.

Collective rights administration, conducted by collecting societies to continuing howls of protest, supplied a workable method of effecting gross revenue transfers. As long as rights holders were remunerated (even though individuals protested that most monies seemed to fill the treasuries of publishers or other producers), politicians felt satisfied that the law fulfilled its function. Whether the transfers were economically efficient or socially justified scarcely bothered policy-makers or legislators.

allowed member nations to limit that control subject to limitations non-injurious to the moral or economic interests of the copyright holder. The Royal Commission had no doubt that institution of a copyright tribunal, while imposing some limitation on the absolute right of the copyright holder to control the broadcast of musical performances, would constitute the type of condition as permitted by the Convention.

The early success of performing right societies in collecting fees from radio stations inspired in copyright producers everywhere a belief that the law should work to guarantee that they were paid for every use made of the material they produced. The industries importuning for privileges usually made common cause before government, and they acknowledged a common principle, that extension of proprietary rights is good for business.

8.6 Producer Copyright

Producer interests, however, are not always reconcilable. The first quarrel between large business factions arose in the early twentieth century between music publishers and the phonographic industry, and resulted—by enactment of a compulsory licence and limited copyright in sound recordings—in the beginnings of the parallel category of analogous producer copyrights.

The justification for this category would be unequivocally utilitarian. Producers' could not claim moral rights and nor could they propose that a postulated natural law demanded that they receive the proprietary protection of copyright. They argued for producer copyrights on grounds distinct from those advanced by the authors' rights advocates, securing exclusive rights never contemplated by the originators of the Berne Convention or the writers, like Victor Hugo or Mark Twain, who argued for new copyright laws.

Protection of investment became the rationale for producer copyrights. Without industries, flourishing markets could not exist; without markets, copyright works would find no audience. Industries, according to this argument, deserved copyright protection no less than creators.

More disingenuously, industries came to argue that without copyright protection, they could not prosper.[11] Underlying their arguments lay a simple imperative: maximize revenue. Copyright, offering monopoly control over production and, to some extent, distribution, seemed to industry leaders an excellent device for dominating markets.

With each other, the mature copyright industries try to maintain peace. But as each groped towards securing copyright protections, the drive for revenue occasionally caused disputes that poisoned commercial relations until accommodations were reached. By the time of the outbreak of the world war in 1914, the music

[11] A presumption disproved by reality: with the exception of the publishing industry, the history of which is entwined with the development of copyright law, all copyright industries grew and generated large profits without the aid of copyright legal protection. The recording, radio and television broadcasting, and software industries expanded rapidly into powerful economic phenomena before they secured copyright protections. The film industry received limited copyright protection in its infancy but film companies had little need to enforce film copyright before the advent of mass copying technology.

publishers and phonographic industry had reached the first such commercial accommodation.

Then, at the beginning of the 1930s, the gramophone industry in the United Kingdom and Australia launched a commercial strike against radio broadcasters, asserting that copyright in recordings comprised a subsidiary copyright in the public performance of records. In 1931, the Gramophone Company and Columbia Gramophone Company (including its subsidiary the Parlophone Company) merged to form a British recording giant, Electrical and Musical Industries Limited, or EMI.[12] EMI's offshoots also controlled the Australian recording scene.

8.7 Radio Ban

EMI regarded radio as a commercial parasite, freely playing records and thus draining from listeners the desire to purchase records. Between 1927 and 1931, record sales fell by a calamitous 80 % and EMI, casting about for causes, blamed music broadcasting for the decline. Radio, declared EMI, released listeners from the necessity of buying records.

They could listen all day to songs—why waste money on records? The company refused to accept that the Great Depression might be the primary cause of its sales catastrophe or that far from undermining sales, radio broadcasts might encourage listeners to buy records. In late 1931, it instituted a boycott against the BBC in Britain and radio broadcasters in Australia, banning them from playing any EMI records.

EMI justified the ban by asserting the record performing right. The radio stations paid public performance fees paid to the PRS and APRA for the right to play the collecting societies' repertoire of musical works. Now, said EMI, they must pay for the right to play the physical recordings of those works—in other words, gramophone records. EMI imposed conditions to the playing of music. The radio stations would be required to discontinue request items, announce the manufacturer and other particulars of the record, specify the manufacturer's reservation of copyright, broadcast only EMI records, restrict the numbers of plays and limit plays of records issued prior to the ban to once a week.

EMI's aggression reaped dividends. Broadcasters were desperate for music and willing to accommodate demands that were economically feasible. The BBC, and in Australia, the national broadcaster, the ABC, agreed to limit the playing of records, and though commercial broadcasters in Australia argued for another two decades over the payment of the record performance fee, they started to meet some of EMI's conditions for the playing of records.

---

[12] In November 2011, Universal Music Group, a subsidiary of Vivendi, bought EMI's music recording business, and a Sony-led conglomerate its music publishing business.

EMI's gambit succeeded in the teeth of official opposition.[13] Policy-makers and legislators rejected the asserted record performing right out of hand. In Australia, the 1933 Royal Commission on the Performing Right disparaged the supposed right. EMI, however, played a long hand, looking to the courts to establish a precedent that it calculated parliament must eventually follow. In 1933, in *Gramophone Co Ltd v. Stephen Cawardine & Co*, Justice Maugham, in Chancery, accepted the recording industry's interpretation of the relevant provision of the British Copyright Act. Record companies, he found, possessed copyright in sound recordings and the right to control public performances—the playing of the records—in public.

Justice Maugham's decision represented a milestone in copyright law as significant as the elaboration of principles of fair use by Justice Story 90 years earlier in *Folsom v. Marsh*. Fair use principles were codified in the 1976 US Copyright Act after becoming so accepted by practitioners and theoreticians of copyright law that, in the eyes of legislators, their enactment merely formalized incontestable legal knowledge.

In the 1930s, few outside the High Court or record industry agreed with Justice Maugham's extrapolation from statute of a record performing right (a right distinct from the performing right of the owner of copyright in the musical work recorded). But 20 years of importuning and advocacy by record companies won politicians to their cause. As Congress would do in 1976, when it incorporated fair use principles in legislation, the British and Australian parliaments codified a common law innovation.

The British *Copyright Act* of 1956 and the Australian Act of 1968 provided for the record performing right, the enactments passing despite strong minority opposition in Parliament. The change in perspective reflected general acceptance that large-scale producers such as the recording industry were entitled to copyright protections analogous to those already given to creators. In the minds of legislators, though not usually in their discourse, investment ranked alongside creativity as grounds for granting proprietary rights.

[13] Radio broadcasts of sound recordings became a mainstay of broadcasts after the introduction of public broadcasting in the 1920s and the advent of electrical methods of the recording process. In 1932, Louis Sterling, a native of the USA and director of EMI, instructed the head of EMI's copyright department to formulate a legal basis for EMI to claim payment for the playing of records by radio broadcasters and to obtain the opinion of the leading copyright lawyer in England in this respect, Stafford Cripps QC (later Labour Party Minister and Chancellor of the Exchequer). Brian Bramall, a young member of EMI's copyright department (in 1953 he became the first Director General of the *International Federation of the Phonographic Industry*—IFPI), wrote to Cripps arguing that the grant of copyright in the record in s. 19(1) of the Copyright Act 1911 comprehended the record performing right. Cripps accepted Bramall's arguments, took the case (*Gramophone Co., Ltd.* v. *Stephen Cawardine & Co.* [1934] Ch. 450, Ch.D.) and won. On the basis of the finding in the case (which was never appealed) that the copyright in the record embraced the right to perform the record in public, Phonogram Performance Limited was founded in 1934 to exercise the right (and continues to do so under the provisions of the Copyright Act 1988). We are indebted to Professor Adrian Sterling of Queen Mary College, University of London and former Deputy Director General of IFPI, for this account.

8.8 US Controversy Over the Public Performance Right

In the United States, during the years when broadcasters in Britain and elsewhere fought performing right societies and the record industry, radio stations and collecting societies occupied the main copyright battleground. The recording industry, like its cousins in Britain and Australia, blamed broadcasting for undermining sales but it found less cause to fight the broadcasters tooth and claw.

Into the 1930s, many radio stations played only live music performed in radio studios by hired musicians and singers. Record companies found it difficult to make a definitive case linking the fall in sales—which occurred consistently with drops in sales of all products during the Depression—and in 1942, the newly formed Capitol Records broke ranks, embracing the so-called 'airplay' of records.

Capitol offered broadcasters a brimming repertoire of songs recorded by new artists, and in 5 years sold over 40 million records. Even before Capitol's inception, the recording industry's boycott of broadcasting, begun in 1932—probably in imitation of EMI's radio ban in Britain and Australia—had come to an end.

Most records sold in the 1930s displayed the legend 'not licensed for broadcast' and lawsuits trying to enforce the prohibition culminated in categoric victory for the broadcasters. In 1940, the federal court ruled that purchase of a record entitled a radio station to play it. A record performance right, recognized by the High Court in England 6 years earlier, did not exist.[14]

Meanwhile, commercial hostilities between ASCAP (the American Society of Authors, Composers and Publishers) and the radio broadcasters continued throughout the interwar years, involving a third protagonist, government. Although often sanguine about ASCAP's near-monopoly over the licensing of copyright music, government would become ASCAP's nemesis.

The battle over the performing right or, rather, fees levied—collections increased from about $380,000 in 1922 (mostly of fees from movie theatres) to about $960,000 at the beginning of the 1930s and $7.3 million in 1940—pitted the standard bearers of the performing right against the nation's most powerful new industry.

Elsewhere in the world, performing right societies, aided by courts that invariably enforced the performance right, irrespective of complaints about its oppressive use, swept aside opposition. Publishing houses were the larger beneficiaries of collections and though they constituted an industrial interest, they made common cause with creators out of necessity—without musical copyrights they could not offer potential licensees like radio stations a repertoire of sanctioned music. In the United States, however, ASCAP, though apparently all-powerful in revenue collection, unknowingly trod a precarious path.

---

[14] *RCA* v. *Whiteman et al.* 114 F 2d 86 (1940).

8.9 ASCAP v. the Radio Industry

The US radio industry, driven by the commercial imperatives of the vast swathe of independent and network stations fighting for market share, fought ASCAP over two decades with a ferocity and resolution never observed among the broadcasters of other continents. And publishers, many already integrated in amalgamated entertainment companies that produced both music and records, were less inclined to identify their economic interests with those of individual copyright holders or a performing right society that shared distributions equally between publishers and composers and lyricists.[15]

The radio stations, represented by the National Association of Broadcasters (NAB), bitterly resented ASCAP's charges, which increased in proportion to revenue and in any case never dropped below 3 % of advertising income.[16] They objected to ASCAP's insistence on issuing blanket licences, which resulted in stations paying fees for songs they never played, its shadowy distribution arrangements and its unwillingness to negotiate licence terms. None of the NAB's objections were unheard of in other parts of the world, which acquiesced sullenly to bullying by performing right societies ever-willing to enforce their will in the courts.

In the United States, however, at the instigation of the NAB, ASCAP's conduct became the subject of scrutiny in the courts and the object of government suspicion. The performing right, wielded with arrogant disdain by ASCAP and its sister organizations throughout the world, ceased to be viewed by courts or politicians as a legal creation above the law. A seemingly unassailable right yielded to a countervailing legal force: anti-trust law.

From the mid-1920s, the NAB lobbied the anti-trust division of the Department of Justice to enforce the Sherman Act to curtail ASCAP's control of collections for the playing of commercial music. The Justice Department vacillated, although ASCAP unquestionably displayed the characteristics of a monopolist, licensing over 80 % of music played on radio and fixing fees with scant regard for broadcasters' financial constraints. The Justice Department, however, like interested government agencies throughout the world, seemed to view collective rights administration as a legitimate exercise of a statutory right and an equitable form of collective bargaining.[17]

---

[15] At the end of 1935, four publishers and their subsidiaries, supposedly controlling about 40 % of ASCAP's in-demand repertoire, withdrew from ASCAP and promised to levy performing right fees independently. The four companies were offshoots of Warner Brothers Pictures, a giant movie-making enterprise formed in 1918. Warner Bros founded Warner Bros Records in 1958. Note that performing right societies in the UK and other countries such as Australia also allocated up to half of revenue collected to artists.

[16] ASCAP demanded increase in royalty volumes of 300 % in 1932 and 70 % in 1937 (Sterling and Kitross 1990).

[17] The effects of the Great Depression, and New Deal politics, may have affected attitudes in the Department of Justice. In the 1930s, the Roosevelt administration seems, in economic affairs, to

In 1933, the NAB took matters into its own hands and asked the federal court to declare ASCAP an unlawful trade combination. Stung into action, a year later the Department of Justice also filed suit, asserting criminal violation of the Sherman Act. The department sought ASCAP's dissolution, but at the court hearing in 1935, the department requested adjournment, possibly because ASCAP and the broadcasters had agreed a provisional 5-year licensing arrangement.[18]

If the combatants reached a compromise agreement, it proved unsatisfactory. Within 2 years, ASCAP announced plans to increase fees by 40 %, and the NAB in any case pursued a strategy of persuading state legislatures to pass their own versions of anti-trust legislation to outlaw ASCAP's activities in the state jurisdictions.

Ten states passed laws prohibiting copyright owners from combining to fix usage fees, but ASCAP struck back, fighting the laws with mixed results in state courts. Ultimately Supreme Court pre-emption declarations killed the NAB's policy. The finding that state legislatures arrogated the federal copyright power invalidated the laws aimed at monopoly and, after years of fighting, seemingly handed the field of revenue collection to ASCAP.[19]

8.10 Anti-Trust

However, seemingly defeated, the NAB now settled on a stratagem that brought ASCAP undone. In 1939, it created its own performing right organization to compete with ASCAP and in doing so changed the nature of popular broadcast American music. The new organization, Broadcast Music Incorporated (BMI), offered radio stations reluctant to sign ASCAP licences a new music repertoire based on genres shunned by ASCAP: rhythm and blues, country, gospel, folk and latin. The success of BMI proved a precursor to the growth of rock 'n' roll and its dissemination across the airwaves.

Just as ASCAP settled down to business as usual, hiking rates by 100 %, BMI—which eschewed blanket licensing[20] in favour of a supposedly more equitable system of paying for the percentage of airtime represented by programme

have concerned itself with amelioration rather than efficiency. Monopoly could be excused on the grounds that it created stability, jobs and revenue.

[18] See Gervais (2010) at 321 f. 44.

[19] *Gibbs* v. *Buck* 307 US 66 (1939) and *Buck* v. *Gallagher* 307 US 95 (1939). For a fuller account of the dispute between the NAB and ASCAP, see Wu (2004). The state laws could also be said to be the result of the usurpation of the federal legislature's constitutional power to make laws regulating commerce.

[20] Blanket licensing provided licensees with the right to play any song in the ASCAP repertoire (although stations only played a fraction of total available songs) in return for payment of a fixed percentage of the licensee's advertising revenue.

plays[21]—offered stations a powerful alternative to ASCAP's plethora of favourites drawn from traditional genres. The big networks controlled by the National Broadcasting Company (NBC), Columbia Broadcasting System (CBS) and Mutual Broadcasting System, themselves involved in the formation of BMI, saw a way to escape the vice created by statute and courts. NBC and CBS broke ranks and signed the BMI licence agreement.

The licence seemed in every way superior to that of ASCAP. Most importantly, it replaced ASCAP's blanket licence with a pay per play payment system. Fees, calculated by reference to sampling survey data, undercut those of ASCAP by a significant margin. BMI did not insist on licence exclusivity. Within 2 years, BMI licensed about three-quarters of radio stations.

Then, in 1941, the big two, NBC and CBS, led a 10-month radio boycott of ASCAP-licensed music. ASCAP folded. To survive, it dropped its royalty demands and slashed its rates. ASCAP and BMI co-existed in the field of music licensing and continue to do so today.

Another factor precipitated ASCAP's collapse. In 1940, the Department of Justice reactivated its interest in prosecuting ASCAP for anti-trust violations. The department's suspicion of ASCAP probably owed something to the lobbying of the NAB and more to government's renewed interest in trust-busting, after a decade spent resuscitating an economy destroyed by overreaching capitalism. In any event, the Department of Justice made clear its opinion that ASCAP's constitution and practice were directed towards monopoly, restraint of trade and price-fixing.

ASCAP vacillated over the department's requirements for non-suit, which included abandoning blanket licensing, and in 1941, the department, having also threatened action against NBC and CBS, entered anti-trust suits against ASCAP and BMI. Both quickly gave way and agreed to consent decrees that compelled them to license music non-exclusively, provide licensees with the option of per-program remuneration and allow members to retain licensing rights. The consent decrees were updated in 1950 and then periodically until the present.[22]

8.11 Summary

Episodes of collective assertion and reaction shaped copyright law in the century between 1850 and 1950. In the early twentieth century, the assertion of authors' rights provoked the furious reaction of the phonographic industry. As a

[21] BMI pioneered the sampling system since adopted by most copyright collecting societies. A comprehensive record or sample of songs broadcast in particular periods supplied a representative snapshot of songs played. Fees were calculated by multiplying per category rates agreed by number of plays of songs. In theory, sampling tied remuneration to actual plays, ensuring accuracy that was absent from the blanket licensing system and preventing overcharging.

[22] The decrees empower certain US courts to act as rate-setting tribunals exercising powers similar to those of copyright tribunals in other jurisdictions such as the UK, Canada and Australia.

consequence, when legislators codified principles of authors' rights, they agreed legislative compromises[23] and their concessions created a tacit principle of non-usurpation.

Legislative gains for authors must not usurp the commercial gains of industries that produce and disseminate copyright material. Conciliation of industries resulted, decades later, in a treaty that created legislative consensus on 'neighbouring rights', analogous copyrights that conferred proprietary rights on industries.[24]

Then, in the years between the world wars, collecting societies aggressively asserted the right of owners of music copyright to demand fees for the public performance of music. Their campaign to extract large fees rom radio broadcasters, the richest source of revenue, caused a bitter reaction from the broadcasting industry. Government intervened and arbitrariness gave way to a degree of conciliation.[25]

In the 1930s, record companies, until now the complacent beneficiaries of legislative accommodations and rich profits, asserted a right to control the public performance of records. They attributed a drastic fall in record sales to the broadcasting of popular recorded music and banned radio stations from playing their records. To general astonishment, the Chancery court in England, presented with the Gramophone Company's arguments, imputed from copyright legislation the record performing right.[26] This *coup de loi* demonstrated how powerfully the contest of commercial interests now influenced copyright law-making.

Each instance of assertion and reaction contributed to the law's transformation from parochial instrument of publishing monopolies to internationally harmonized system for enforcing authorial control over the production and dissemination of copyright works. Such a system could not find favour unless it accommodated the requirements of industries unwilling to let creators usurp control of their functions. The process of accommodation inevitably involved departure from principle, but so too did the programme of authors' rights.

As can be discerned from the preambles to the first copyright legislation passed in the United Kingdom and United States, and the content of successive legislation passed before the twentieth century, copyright law-makers before the twentieth century tried to give effect to a principle of public benefit.

---

[23] In the form of statutory provision for the compulsory recording licence and species of copyrights in records and films.

[24] *International Convention for the Protection of Performers, Producers of Phonograms and Broadcasting Organizations*, Rome 1961 (Rome Convention).

[25] The essential legal reform eventually instituted by most governments involved legislative provision for courts or tribunals to determine, in the parlance of Berne-affiliated nations, 'equitable remuneration' for public performances.

[26] The US legislature did not recognize the record performing right and by the time of its enactment in Britain's 1956 Copyright Act, the record and radio industries were making peace. Record companies recognized that broadcasting, far from hurting profits, created sales momentum, turning favoured releases into smash hits and helping the record companies to sell millions of records.

The law, so far as most of them were concerned, existed to guarantee the supply of literature. It did so by granting authors, or their factotums, publishers, exclusive control over supply. Enforceable rights, lasting for a restricted period, protected producers against piracy and ensured that their margins could support continued production.

In the twentieth century, developments in copyright law owed little to this principle of regulation. The convulsive expansion of the law's scope resulted in statutory regimes that were only in a remote sense derivatives of laws invented 'for the encouragement of learning'. Statutes that enabled authors and industries to profit from playing music over the airwaves, or the sale of records, or the performance of films, differed in policy, as well as character, from earlier legislation.

Law-makers seemed scarcely to consider whether protection truly lasted only for as long as necessary to protect investment or laws encouraged dissemination, or conversely, opened doors to profiteering or commercial oppression. In the twentieth century, copyright law functioned not to encourage dissemination by protecting investment, but to facilitate revenue transfers. Technology for recording and broadcasting music, enabling millions to listen to records and radio, changed utterly the expectations and strategies of copyright holders.

By 1950, copyright law regulated a new economic system based on mass consumption and publishers, record companies and film producers stepped into the foreground of the copyright stage. They derived revenue from taxing consumption and since the audiences numbered in the millions, their revenues grew in multiples unimaginable when the copyright law functioned to allow book publishers to regulate supply.

In the rush to profit, serious discussion of the purpose of copyright law—clearly articulated by legislators in the eighteenth century—became largely excluded from legal discourse. After 1950, the concern with extending the law to permit taxation of use ensured that the copyright rubric governed the application of new technologies for reproduction or dissemination. Legal controversy rarely involved questions about the social utility or economic efficiency of existing rights, or proposed extensions. Enlargement of rights to permit taxation of use became a dynamic principle, motivating copyright advocates and legislators alike.

References

Gervais D (ed) (2010) Collective management of copyright and related rights, 2nd edn. Wolters Kluwer, Austin

Sterling CH, Kitross JM (1990) Stay tuned: a concise history of American broadcasting, 2nd edn. Wadsworth C, Belmont

Vaidhyanathan S (2001) Copyrights and copywrongs: the rise of intellectual property and how it threatens creativity. New York University Press, New York

Wu T (2004) Copyright's communications policy. Michigan Law Rev 278: pp. 89

Chapter 9
UNESCO, The UCC and Copyright Access

9.1 Third Phase of Copyright Law Development

The years after 1950 might reasonably be referred to as the third phase of development of international copyright law. During the 150 years following the enactment of the Statute of Anne in 1710, the semblance of a philosophy of copyright emerged to accompany the appearance of legislation in countries like the United States and France. Whether legislatures passed laws ostensibly to encourage learning (the United Kingdom and United States) or to recognize inalienable personal rights (France), all acknowledged the author as a figure of social value, deserving of reward.

A second phase occurred from the middle to the late nineteenth century. Internationalism, permeated with the values of the authors' rights movement, established the character of copyright law throughout the globe. In the twentieth century, the law regulated far more than the economic transactions of publishers, extending its reach to govern music recording and the public performance of music by radio broadcasters. Although the music and radio broadcasting industries were yet to procure rights co-extensive with those enjoyed by authors, the rising conflict between the economic priorities of industries and authors would shortly contribute to the third phase of regulatory growth.

After 1950, a new internationalism—shaped first by the post-war politics of decolonization and, later, by the politics of economic hegemony—transformed international copyright law into an instrument favourable to the export needs of the entertainment, broadcasting and software industries of the United States. The central role played by the US in regulatory developments reflected more than global demand for the products of its copyright industries. It owed much to the primary position of the US in world economic affairs, an ascendancy manifest in the extraordinary achievements of Silicon Valley.

From the 1940s, streams of creative scientific endeavour—uncontained by copyright rules—created the US software industry, and the beginnings of networked communication. The 1976 US Copyright Act established copyright in

B. Atkinson and B. Fitzgerald, *A Short History of Copyright*,
DOI 10.1007/978-3-319-02075-4_9, © Springer International Publishing Switzerland 2014

computer programs and thereafter began the contest that runs to the present day between the advocates for greater or lesser copyright control over digital communication. Digital communication, and the development of the internet, has transformed the landscape of the copyright world, perhaps more pervasively than sound recording and radio and television broadcasting.

It has brought to the forefront of consciousness a third force in copyright politics: the public, long neglected by legislators in favour of private and corporate interest. The public desire for access to information of all types, the extent to which politicians and copyright holders insist on control over information supply and the degree to which conflicting—or merely different—interests negotiate terms of information access are factors likely to determine the viability of copyright law in the future.

9.2 Developments in International Law

In 1952, representatives of 36 members of the United Nations Educational, Scientific and Cultural Organization (UNESCO) signed the Universal Copyright Convention (UCC). They intended the UCC to 'ensure respect for the rights of the individual and encourage the development of literature, the sciences and the arts', and to 'facilitate a wider dissemination[1] and increase international understanding'.[2] This event ushered in a new age of syncretism, as legislators tried to reconcile the claims of creators, producers and public.[3]

Their efforts gave rise to the axiom that copyright regulation exists to 'balance' the interests of the owners and users of copyright material.[4] Legislation created, in the form of specific exemptions from the operation of exclusive rights, entitlement

[1] Cf. *Convention Establishing the World Intellectual Property Organization* 1967, Article (vi): '[WIPO] shall assemble and disseminate information concerning the protection of intellectual property, carry out and promote studies in this field, and publish the results of such studies.' The Berne Convention does not refer to dissemination.

[2] These phrases form part of the preamble of the UCC signed by 36 nations on 6 September 1952. Formed as an agency of the United Nations in 1945, UNESCO's stated purpose is 'to contribute to peace and security by promoting collaboration among the nations through education, science and culture in order to further universal respect for justice, for the rule of law and for . . . human rights and fundamental freedoms' (Article 1.1 UNESCO constitution, adopted 16 November 1945). The preamble states that 'since wars begin in the minds of men, it is in the minds of men that the defences of peace must be constructed'.

[3] Signatories to the UCC included the US, a large number of Berne Union members and nearly 30 South American, Asian and African countries that were not signatories to the Berne Convention.

[4] This was first officially stated in the Australian *Spicer Committee Report* (Report of the Committee Appointed to Consider What Alterations Are Desirable in the Copyright Law of the Commonwealth 1959) and repeated regularly in general copyright literature.

to free, or fair, use of copyright material.[5] Copyright advocates cited free use provisions in legislation as evidence that the law did not invariably regulate output for the benefit of industries and exporters. Copying that did not undermine the profits of copyright owners could, in certain circumstances, be deemed lawful.[6]

The logic of exclusive rights, however, precluded much limitation. Syncretic gloss could not hide the reality that, in practice, international copyright law functioned principally to protect the profits of industries. Leading members of the Berne Convention, and signatories of copyright treaties signed in the 1990s,[7] did not in principle oppose UNESCO's policy of encouraging 'wider dissemination'. But these treaties—the WIPO treaties and TRIPS Agreement—increased the scope and coercive effect of international copyright law, frustrating hopes that governments would support permissive policies concerning access to copyright material.

9.3 The UCC

The UCC, and the changes it portended for international copyright law, resulted from post-war determination to create an international order based on equitable relations, openness and exchange of knowledge.[8] UNESCO's policy for about

[5] In the United Kingdom, the old law of fair abridgement ultimately found its way, in modified form, to the statute books (beginning with the 1911 Copyright Act) as fair dealing, which, like the US fair use doctrine, permits free use of copyright material subject to a user satisfying certain criteria. UK legislation, like that of other common law countries such as Australia, permits fair dealing for specified purposes, such as research and study. The founding case on fair use in the US is *Folsom* v. *Marsh* 9 F.Cas. 342 (1841).

[6] The literature on fair use is copious, and expresses wide divergence of opinion on the doctrine's utility and value. See, for example, Gordon (1982).

[7] *Agreement on Trade-Related Aspects of Intellectual Property Rights* (TRIPS), negotiated in the 1986–1994 Uruguay Round of talks on the General Agreement on Trade and Tariffs, Annex 1C of Marrakesh Agreement creating the World Trade Organization; WIPO Copyright Treaty 1996 (WCT) and WIPO Performances and Phonograms Treaty 1996 (WPPT).

[8] The genesis of UNESCO lay in wartime meetings of Allied educational ministers who recommended in 1945 that the United Nations create an educational and cultural organization to help create a new moral and intellectual order for humanity. Dedicated to help spread through the world the benefits of peace, security, justice, education and respect for human rights and human freedoms enunciated in the Charter of the UN, UNESCO expressed a moral vision different from that of the Berne Convention. It could only be expected that the framers of the UCC would adopt an attitude friendlier to public interest than that of the founders and supporters of the Berne Convention, which contains no preamble asserting the public interest in dissemination. On the other hand, it should be remembered that the Berne Union collaborated closely with UNESCO and the UCC's intergovernmental committee on issues concerning developing countries in the 1960s and 1970s.

20 years after the UCC came into being emphasized that copyright law must work to spread, rather than hoard, knowledge.[9]

In this aspect, policy prefigured contemporary movements in favour of public access to information.[10] Philosophically, by encouraging public dissemination, UNESCO diverged from the Berne Union, which proselytized for authors' rights, and thus upheld the discretion of proprietors to withhold, restrict or otherwise control the supply of information.

The UCC set out a scheme of copyright standards that were less prescriptive than the Berne Convention, although more demanding in relation to formalities. Obligations were general not specific: member states were to provide 'adequate and effective protection' of copyright works. Members must comply with simple formalities before they could take advantage of protection under the convention: owners were required to affix to works the © symbol, specify the copyright holder's name and state the year of first publication.

The UCC suggested to developing nations that were members of the Berne Union the possibility of demanding special rights that recognized their developmental needs.[11] For the first time, international copyright forums began to recognize the existence of a generalized, transnational 'user' interest. At the close of the 1950s, the UCC's intergovernmental committee, as well as UNESCO's general conference, began considering the access needs of poorer countries. In 1960, they agreed that the intergovernmental committee should examine ways to deliver educational books cheaply to underdeveloped countries.

9.4 Brazzaville

In 1963, representatives of interested African countries attended a meeting on copyright legislative policy at Brazzaville, capital of the Republic of the Congo. Organized jointly by the UCC and the Berne Union, the meeting supposedly continued the programme of the UCC intergovernmental copyright committee, allowing African nations to highlight the retrograde effects on development of copyright restrictions and suggest ways to alleviate these effects.[12]

---

[9] This is reflected in the initiative, lasting for about a decade from the late 1950s, and involving the Berne Union, to negotiate on behalf of less developed countries privileges permitting access to copyright material published in the developed world.

[10] The movements (free software, open source, creative commons, Wikimedia, peer-to-peer and so on) stress the importance of users exercising their freedom to allow copying and modification of their work without significant proprietary restriction. The resulting flow of information creates a 'commons' of information freely accessible to the public.

[11] The literature on the UCC is surprisingly sparse, and accounts of its purpose differ. Some observers depict it as an instrument designed to bring the United States into the mainstream of international law and eventually the Berne Union. See Ringer (1968), pp. 1055–1062; Jaszi (1989), pp. 47–72; Yu (2004), pp. 323–443.

[12] See 'General Report of the Brazzaville Session' [1963] *RIDA*, Vol. 1.

To the consternation of Western delegates schooled in catechisms of authors' rights and, more recently, neighbouring rights, African representatives declared the necessity for exemptions from international law far beyond any contemplated by Western governments. Africans wanted, above all, reduced periods of copyright protection and rights to copy and abridge imported copyright works, without charge, for the purpose of education.

The African nations, supported by India and other developing nations, were unimpressed by the doctrine of authors' rights, which, though it honoured creative moral entitlement, seemed to them to strengthen the economic interests of Western publishers. At this stage, the existence of the UCC, and the apparent activism of UNESCO, pointed to the possibility of an alternative copyright movement supplanting the influence of Berne.

Delegates of the Berne Union, who were sensitive to the political currents generated by decolonization, tried to accommodate the complaints of developing nations; publishers and authors from Europe (and the United States) did not. By the time of the 1967 Berne Convention revision conference, held in Stockholm, they had resolved to oppose the Brazzaville manifesto of special needs.

9.5 Access Rights

At the Stockholm conference, a committee of experts proposed that developing countries be allowed to apply to make reservations to the Convention on grounds of economic, scientific, social and cultural needs. Reservations, applicable for a fixed period, could include the right to use works free of charge for scholastic purposes. Delegates from developed nations reluctantly lent support and the conference adopted a Convention protocol allowing developing nations special licensing and translation rights.[13]

Publisher groups, however, would not accept the protocol[14] and some government delegates, especially those of Britain, and official observers, especially those of the United States, shared their views.[15] Their united opposition to special needs

[13] Developing nations were not obliged to protect the copyright of a foreign author for more than a posthumous period of 25 years. They could allow local interests to make unauthorized translations of untranslated foreign works and publish translations. Most importantly, they could license local interests to copy foreign literary and artistic works for teaching, study and research purposes. See Berne Convention for the Protection of Literary and Artistic Works, revised Stockholm 14 July 1967, *Protocol Regarding Developing Countries*, entry into force 29 January/26 February 1970.

[14] For example, the International Publishers Association domiciled in Geneva and the International Group of Scientific, Technical & Medical Publishers, founded in 1968 in Amsterdam to, among other things, lobby for copyright protection.

[15] British publishing representatives were in the vanguard of opposition to the idea of special needs. US observers included the future Register of Copyrights, Barbara Ringer, a key influence on the content of the 1976 US Copyright Act.

ensured that the Stockholm protocol entered the world stillborn. At their instigation, representatives of the newly created World Intellectual Property Organization (administrator of the Berne Convention)[16] and UNESCO supplied the machinery to implement a compromise arrangement chiefly influenced by the publishers of developed nations. In 1971, joint revision conferences for the UCC and Berne Convention permitted developing countries to reprint and translate foreign works under restricted compulsory licence.[17] Restrictions ensured benefits were illusory.[18]

The fierce response to proposals to exempt poorer countries from copying prohibitions, even though privileges were intended to assist in education, ended, for practical purposes, UNESCO's ambition for international copyright law to evolve into an instrument of dissemination. The prestige of the Berne Convention grew while that of the UCC diminished.[19] The publishers' strategy to end controversy over the special needs of poorer countries worked, although Brazil and Argentina issued fresh calls for access rights in 2004.[20]

---

[16] WIPO, an agency of the United Nations, came into being in 1967, succeeding BIRPI, or the Bureau Internationaux Réunis pour la Protection de la Propriété Intellectuelle, the administrator of the Berne Convention. WIPO is empowered 'in order to encourage creative activity, to promote the protection of intellectual property throughout the world' (Preamble para 2).

[17] The conferences were held in Paris in 1971 and amendments took effect (after sufficient ratification) in 1974.

[18] A developing country's central copyright agency could issue a licence if the originating publisher:

- Enjoyed the exclusive reproduction right in the jurisdiction for specific periods (3–7 years for copies, 1–3 years for translations)
- Did not offered works for sale in the jurisdiction at a reasonable price
- Did not respond to publisher requests for voluntary licences, or refused to grant a licence for consideration.

Restrictions favoured foreign publishers, who could dispute the grounds on which a licence might be claimed. The requirement to pay royalties approximate to those payable under voluntary licences, the limited educational purposes for which licensed material could be published and the prohibition on selling material for profit discouraged local publishers from applying for licences. See Berne Convention, Paris Text, 24 July 1971, Appendix [concerning Developing Countries].

[19] UNESCO worked closely with the WIPO in the 1960s to 1980s and, increasingly, the latter, a specialist United Nations agency, assumed a naturally dominant role in international copyright policy formation. Its larger membership, more ready alignment with the economic goals of powerful producer interests and, increasingly, greater specialist expertise ensured that its voice became dominant in international discussion.

[20] Brazil and Argentina's representatives presented to the WIPO General Assembly the WIPO *Development Agenda*. The Development Agenda challenges assumptions about the benefits of implementing rigorous intellectual property (IP) legal regimes in developing countries. It calls for adoption of a 'development agenda' in international IP policy-making and proposes a treaty to, among other things, promote access to publicly funded research in developed countries. In 2007, WIPO established a Development Agenda and a related Committee on Development and Intellectual Property (CDIP). The CDIP is charged with monitoring, implementing and discussing WIPO's development programme. In May 2013, the CDIP agreed to continue work towards implementation of the 45 recommendations adopted by the WIPO General Assembly in 2007. At the meeting, Brazil, on behalf of the Development Agenda Group, expressed concern

9.6 Cultural Expression of Indigenous People

Although in the 1970s WIPO seemed uninterested in an access-to-knowledge programme based on recognition of special needs, the agency focused attention on protection of folklore and traditional knowledge. In 1978, a joint WIPO-UNESCO council agreed guidelines for WIPO members to protect folklore with national laws in their jurisdictions.[21] Guidelines affirmed that the right of indigenous people to self-determination comprehended protection of their culture. Some observers drew a connection with the development needs of less developed nations. They argued that protection of culture, including traditional knowledge, is indispensable to securing economic growth and avoiding environmental degradation (see Verma 2004).

Progress on protection of folklore and traditional knowledge, or the more encompassing category of protection known as traditional cultural expression, proved, for advocates, frustratingly slow. In the 1990s, the United Nations High Commissioner for Human Rights and WIPO sponsored declarations recognizing the intellectual property rights of indigenous people,[22] and in 2007 WIPO published 'Draft Provisions on the Protection of Traditional Cultural Expressions/Folklore and Traditional Knowledge'.[23] However, as one paper has noted, until WIPO's legislative proposals are implemented in jurisdictions around the world, traditional cultural expressions remain vulnerable to proprietary (and non-proprietary) appropriation.[24]

---

that some WIPO members were not maintaining commitment to effective implementation of the *Development Agenda.*

[21] WIPO-UNESCO Committee of Governmental Experts, 'Model Provisions for National Laws on the Protection of Expressions of Folklore against Illicit Exploitation and other Prejudicial Actions' (1982).

[22] UNCHR Sub-Commission o[n] Prevention of Discrimination and Protection of Minorities Working Group on Indigenous Populations, *Mataatua Declaration on the Cultural and Intellectual Property Rights of Indigenous Peoples*, First International Conference on the Cultural and Intellectual Property Rights of Indigenous Peoples, 12–18 June 1993, Whakatane (NZ), (Commission on Human Rights, WIPO, 1993);UNHCHR, Sub-Commission on Prevention of Discrimination and Protection of Minorities (renamed Sub-Commission on the Promotion and Protection of Human Rights in 1999), *Draft Declaration of the Rights of Indigenous Peoples* (United Nations, 1994, adopted by the General Assembly in 2007). See also OCHR Leaflet No 12, *WIPO and Indigenous People* (www.ohchr.org/Documents/Publications/GuideIPleaflet12en.pdf).

[23] Available at www.wipo/int/tk/en/consultations/draft_provisions/draft_provisions.html (8 March 2007).

[24] Fitzgerald and Hedge (2008).

References

Fitzgerald B, Hedge S (2008) Traditional cultural expression and the internet world. In: Antons C (ed) Traditional knowledge, traditional cultural expression and intellectual property in South East Asia. Kluwer, Dordrecht, http://eprints.qut.edu.au/13675

Gordon W (1982) Fair use as market failure: a structural and economic analysis of the "Betamax" case and its predecessors. Columb Law Rev 82(8):1600–1659

Jaszi P (1989) A garland of reflections on three international copyright topics. Cardozo Arts Entertain Law J 8:47–72

Ringer B (1968) The role of the United States in international copyright – past, present, and future. Georget Law J 56:1055–1062

Spicer Committee (1959) Report of the committee appointed by the Attorney-General of the commonwealth to consider what alterations are desirable in the copyright law of the commonwealth, Commonwealth of Australia, Canberra

Verma SK (2004) Protecting traditional knowledge: is a sui generis system an answer? J World Intellect Prop 7(6):765–805

Yu PK (2004) Currents and crosscurrents in the international intellectual property regime (symposium: intellectual property at a crossroads). Loyola Los Angel Law Rev 38:323–443

Chapter 10
A Right to Payment, Neighbouring Rights and the Merits of Copyright

10.1 Photocopying

The possibility of less developed nations adopting compulsory copying licences caused alarm to Western publishers, since unremunerated copying threatened profits in secondary markets. Though smaller in scale than those in developed countries, markets in poorer countries were still valuable sources of income. Having disposed of one perceived threat, publishers turned their attention to another menace, as they saw it.

By the mid-1960s, they knew that as photocopiers spread to libraries and offices around the world, schoolchildren, university students and workers would copy hundreds of millions of pages of published works. Publishers were not interested in suppression. They wished to regulate photocopying, and collect fees for copying.[1]

For another decade, publishers brooded as around the world students and employees copied pages of published works. How, they asked themselves, could they subvert the magic of the new machines and restore harmony to a universe in which nothing is for free? Eventually, they undid the spell, and the world accepted the principle that fractional copying—the copying of single, or multiple, pages of a work—must be remunerated.

The *International Publishers Association*, the *International Federation for Documentation*, the *International Federation of Library Associations* and many others pressed governments to take action on their behalf. As early as 1961, an expert joint subcommittee of the UCC's intergovernmental copyright committee and the Berne Union's executive committee started 'to formulate recommendations for possible

[1] According to evidence presented to the US House Committee on the Judiciary (Subcommittee no 3, June, August–September 1965), in the preceding year copying machines in the US produced 9.5 billion copies of document pages.

B. Atkinson and B. Fitzgerald, *A Short History of Copyright*,
DOI 10.1007/978-3-319-02075-4_10,

solutions'.[2] Subcommittee deliberations continued for over two decades until the group of experts[3] affirmed in 1984 that the Berne Convention and UCC granted authors exclusive control over all aspects of reproduction, including private copying for non-commercial purposes.[4]

By this time a number of countries had established compulsory licences for photocopying[5] and, subsequently, WIPO encouraged the founding in member countries of reproduction rights organizations (RROs) to license photocopying of scientific and cultural works.[6]

Copyright industries asserted a near-total power of proscription. Allowing for the narrow range of statutory exceptions, the exclusive rights, so they said, permitted them to forbid all types of copying, regardless of the purpose of copying or the identity of the copier. They took for granted that the proscription power included a right to remuneration. If the copyright owner could forbid an activity, then the owner could demand payment as the condition for permitting the activity.[7]

10.2 Right to Remuneration

The radical aspect of presuming a remuneration right lies in stepping beyond the literal meaning of exclusive rights. The right to prohibit enables the copyright holder to negotiate payment, not to compel payment. However, compulsory licensing schemes, created at the behest of government for the benefit of music and print publishers, introduced compulsion into copyright transactions and taxation of a

[2] Report prepared by secretariats of UNESCO and Berne Union on meeting of Committee of Experts on the Photographic Reproduction of Protected Works, Paris 1–5 July 1968.

[3] Group of Experts on the Private Copying of Protected Works appointed by the subcommittee of the executive committee of the Berne Union (WIPO) in 1975.

[4] The Group of Experts' finding on photocopying in 1984 resulted in WIPO appointing a committee of experts in 1987 to draft model legislative provisions relating to photocopying. The committee met in 1989. See the related Council of Europe Committee of Ministers, recommendation 11, 25 April 1990, *On Principles Relating to Copyright Law Questions in the Field of Reprography*.

[5] Sweden and the Netherlands introduced the first compulsory licensing schemes for photocopying in 1972. The Swedish scheme involved government compensating publishers for educational copying, and the Netherlands scheme, promulgated first by law and then by administrative decrees, required public and educational institutions to pay publishers prescribed rates for copying. Commercial enterprises were required to negotiate 'equitable' remuneration.

[6] RROs are represented in international fora by the International Federation of Reproduction Rights Organisations founded in 1988. See WIPO National Seminar on Copyright, Related Rights and Collective Management, Khartoum, WIPO/CR/KRT/05/6 (RROs paper), January 2005.

[7] This argument, with one difference, mirrored that of the performing right societies, which, decades earlier, insisted that the public performance right empowered them to extract public performance fees. Unlike the print publishers, the performing right societies demanded payment for musical performance of whole works, not units of work.

wide range of non-commercial users—radio listeners, students, government employees.[8]

Publishers insisted that economic value subsisted in each page copied. They pressed the view that each unauthorized copy of a page germinated seeds of economic harm. Governments, WIPO, UNESCO, all accepted that unremunerated fractional copying harmed copyright holders. Government reprographic inquiries failed to test the publishers' thesis and publishers responded by turning the demand for remuneration into an article of necessity.

Official acceptance, in the 1970s, of the proposition that, subject to exceptions, each copy is remunerable profoundly altered attitudes to using, and paying for the use of, copyright material.

Policy-makers accepted that copyright bestowed a right to remuneration. If the explicit right to prohibit comprehended an implicit right to payment, proprietors could expect remuneration for any kind of copying or public performance.[9] Copyright industries fervently repeated the message that use must be compensated, conflating copying and piracy.

Government thus accepted the fallacy of intrinsic value, the premise that fractions of a work, such as the contents of a page, are intrinsically valuable, and their value realizable in a market. In so doing, they paved the way for the coming wars over peer-to-peer copying on the internet. As defenders of peer-to-peer activities discovered, government and industries rejected the argument that private copying or file-sharing may have no effect on existing or future markets.[10]

10.3 Neighbouring Rights

The second half of the twentieth century could loosely be called an era of industrial domination in copyright affairs, just as the first half of the century might be seen as decades in which authors' rights preoccupied official thinking. The so-called copyright industries—entertainment, broadcasting and software industries—

[8] A distinction should be drawn between compulsory licensing schemes for music recording and the public performance of musical works and compulsory licences for photocopying. The recording and public performance licences, introduced in the first four decades of the twentieth century, were aimed at industries using copying material for commercial benefit. The photocopying licence taxed predominantly non-commercial copiers.

[9] In 1961, the International Convention for the Protection of Performers, Producers of Phonograms and Broadcasting Organizations (the Rome Convention) provided in Article 12 (Secondary Use of Phonograms) that users who broadcast phonograms must remunerate the producers of the phonograms (and/or performers of the material recorded on the phonogram).

[10] The WIPO *Performances and Phonograms Treaty* 1996 (Article 15) establishes a remuneration right for performers and phonogram producers, for the use of phonograms to broadcast or communicate to the public (and/or performers of the material recorded on the phonogram).

became increasingly vociferous and assertive in government and public forums, pressing hard for legal advantages.[11]

They protected their interests with great strategic acumen, but to a significant degree they owed the copyrights bestowed on them to the concentrated efforts of lawyers in civil law countries (and also Berne Union delegates) who sought to distinguish clearly between the natural rights of authors and positive rights of industries.

The neighbouring rights movement grew from attempts in civil law countries to resolve practical difficulties caused by the legal conception of copyright as a personal right, an entitlement available to natural persons, not corporations. Lawyers acknowledged that if copyright is understood as the legal distillation of authors' rights, then its protections could not extend to corporations that made recordings or broadcasts of copyright works, or to individuals who performed works. They asserted that corporations or performers possessed *neighbouring* rights—rights analogous to those of copyright holders and equally deserving of proprietary protection.[12]

Berne Convention amendment conferences viewed the issue of neighbouring rights with increasing disquiet, since an instrument devoted to authors' rights could not easily accommodate proposals that sought for industries' recognition of their claims to copyright protection. In 1948, the Berne Convention's Brussels amendment conference resolved that claims of industries must be examined separately by experts and perhaps satisfied by treaty. Meetings of experts gave way in 1957 to a joint committee of experts convened by UNESCO and the Berne Union. The committee's draft agreement (the Monaco draft) formed the basis for a final agreement reached after a diplomatic conference in Rome in 1960.

In 1961, in Rome, the United International Bureau for the Protection of Intellectual Property, UNESCO and the International Labour Organization joined to establish the *International Convention for the Protection of Performers, Producers of Phonograms and Broadcasting Organizations*, signed by 40 states. The Rome Convention established the right of record producers to authorize or prevent unauthorized direct or indirect reproduction of phonograms, and broadcaster rights

[11] The Berne Convention, which guided international law-making in the first half of the century, delinked the primary rights of authors and secondary rights of industries (the compulsory recording licence, sound and film copyrights, permission to members to legislate to place limitations on the author's broadcasting right). Assertive lobbying for neighbouring rights began in the second half of the century, leading to agreement of the Rome Convention in 1961 and recognition, in the United Kingdom and Australia, of the record performing right (1956 and 1968). The *International Federation of the Phonographic Industry* (IFPI) was particularly effective in lobbying for acceptance of a record performing right in the 1960s to1980s. In the US (and internationally), the *International Intellectual Property Alliance*, formed in 1984, has proved effective in lobbying governments to institute legislative reforms designed to strengthen industries' copyrights and facilitate rights enforcement.

[12] Austria passed legislation in 1936 creating 'related rights' of performers, broadcasters and the producers of film and sound recordings. Italy followed suit in 1941 and Scandinavian countries in the 1960s.

to authorize or prohibit rebroadcasts and their recording.[13] Performers received the right to prevent unauthorized fixation or broadcasting of performances.

In 1971, the Phonograms Convention,[14] created by WIPO and UNESCO at the behest of the international recording industry, obliged members to prohibit unauthorized reproduction and the importation of unauthorized reproductions for distribution to the public. Although the United States declined to join the Rome Convention, US industries, like their European counterparts, saw clearly the benefit of proprietary control over reproduction and dissemination of copyright material.[15]

10.4 Supremacy of Property-Based Assumptions

By the 1990s, the UCC was a neglected accord, and copyright proponents reaffirmed the Berne Convention as the preferable compact. The burst of growth in international law towards the close of the twentieth century benefitted certain US industries, by far the greatest exporters, and disseminators, of copyright product. Giving confidence to those industries, WIPO and the World Trade Organization (WTO) controlled the machinery for administering international law and enforcing rights asserted in trade disputes.[16]

By the end of the century, private rather than public benefit influenced the planning of policy-makers. In the 1990s, the collapse of communism in the Soviet Union and Eastern Europe presaged the supremacy, in intellectual discourse, of absolute conceptions of possessory rights. Since the demise of communism seemed to disprove the Marxist promise that societies could be constituted propertyless, many took for granted that theories declaring proprietary rights contingent were now also discredited. Politicians accepted the idea, advanced by thinkers before and since Locke, that ingenuity and labour create entitlement to ownership, and that restriction of this entitlement also restricts liberty.

---

[13] The Convention did not create a record performing right for producers of phonograms but it did establish a right of remuneration for broadcasting of phonograms (Article 12).

[14] WIPO Convention for the Protection of Producers of Phonograms against Unauthorized Duplication of their Phonograms, Geneva, 29 October 1971.

[15] Lobbied intensively by the US recording industry, the US government signed the Phonograms Convention in 1971, the same year in which Congress recognized sound recording copyright. The US decided against signing the Rome Convention primarily because broadcasters objected to Article 12 requiring broadcasters to pay fees for broadcasting records.

[16] The WTO, created in 1994, administers the TRIPS Agreement, and provides a disputes resolution forum for resolving trade disputes brought concerning alleged non-compliance with TRIPS obligations. The Dispute Settlement Board has established extensive jurisprudence since 1994. Two key copyright cases involved disputes between the major trade jurisdictions. See *EC* v. *USA* (2000) – *United States – section 110(5) of US Copyright Act* re payment of royalties for public performance of music; *United States* v. *China* (2009) – *Measures affecting the Protection and Enforcement of Intellectual Property Rights* re, among other things, denial of copyright and related rights protection.

Whatever crumbs of comfort they scattered to the supplicants for 'wider dissemination', they continued to oversee the long march of privatization. In the 1990s, the efforts of WIPO, and diplomatic coteries led by the United States, ensured that international copyright law regulated processes of digital communication.[17] The exclusive rights now extended to all conceivable ways of reproducing and distributing copyright material. In theory, nearly every use of copyright material could be declared remunerable.[18] From now onwards, it seemed, the relationship between supplier and consumer of copyright material must in most instances be mercenary.

The twentieth century thus ended in apotheosis, as copyright law solidified a scheme of rights that expressed in full the credo of entitlement announced by eighteenth-century booksellers in Edinburgh and London. They, following John Locke, identified property in works as the natural, and thus inextinguishable, consequence of creative effort. Two and a half centuries later, when pressed, supporters of copyright also defended rights by appeal to nature. Copyright law, they stated, or implied, justified itself. Whatever could be defined could be owned, and nature, as much as social utility, obliged the state to protect whatever is owned from the depredations of pirates, free-riders and 'thieves'.

10.5 Digital Lawlessness

In the twenty-first century, the beneficiaries of copyright's world order discovered that injunctions, penalties and willing courts could not guarantee what the laws plainly enabled: generation of super-profits. Digital technology, which made possible internet commerce and the creation of worldwide markets for digital products, also facilitated unauthorized mass copying of digital works and products, and electronic distribution of illicit copies.

The film and music industries feared a particular threat to the copyright leviathan: the internet. The willingness of tens of millions of prospective consumers to use file-sharing software to download unauthorized copies of videos or music caused the industries to embark on a decade of legal warfare against practices that they characterized as theft of their property. Courts usually upheld the industry lawsuits as they must: unauthorized copying of works in digital format transparently infringed the literal text of copyright law.

[17] The WIPO Copyright Treaty 1996 created a right of communication to the public (Article 8) that vested in copyright holders the right to authorize 'any communication to the public of their works ... including making available to the public of their works in such a way that members of the public may access these works from a place and at a time individually chosen by them'. The WIPO Performances and Phonograms Treaty 1996 refers (Articles 10 and 14) to the right of making available ('making available to the public').

[18] Although the legitimacy of claims that offer no criteria for determining the harm caused by copyright use is open to doubt.

Varieties of textual and doctrinal literalism characterized arguments over so-called peer-to-peer copying. While lawyers cited the defence of fair use (alleging in substance that copying for private purposes caused no economic harm to copyright holders), neither they, nor copyright thinkers, adopted a plastic view of exclusive rights. They failed to make the case that, historically, legislatures did not intend courts to censure unauthorized copying that does not undermine the proprietor's market.[19]

A decade of litigiousness yielded small comfort to the industries. The continued proliferation of internet file-sharing sites and willingness of a multiplying legion of internet users to download illicit copies of material emphasized the powerlessness of copyright proprietors to enforce rights infringed by scattered millions. The industries' problem of enforcement attracted the sympathy of governments, the agencies of international law and legislators, but enactment in legislation of criminal provisions, and draconian penalties, failed to stem the tide of lawlessness.

10.6 Merits of Copyright

As argument raged in the twenty-first century over the scale of economic damage caused by peer-to-peer infringement, public debate concentrated on the thorny question of justification. If millions of otherwise law-abiding citizens felt unconstrained to violate copyright laws, were the laws fair or reasonable? Copyright defenders responded that unauthorized copying or downloading is theft, since each reproduction made of the owner's property is appropriation of that property. They declared the act of reproduction identical, in principle, to theft of a tangible object.

This dialectic of transgression ignored a truth too disconcerting for copyright industries to contemplate: if laws disobeyed are not enforceable, they lapse into redundancy or must be renegotiated. In the interim, economic interests protected by property rights may be radically harmed. Industries refused negotiation but resort to moral argument, insistence that illegal copying is theft, did not prevent public focus on the content of copyright laws.[20]

One hundred and fifty years after the death of the French anarchist Pierre-Joseph Proudhon, critics of copyright power, repeated, in effect, Proudhon's famous question, *what is property*? (1840/1994). By what right, divine, natural or positive, does a person own anything? While few went so far as Proudhon, who answered

[19] For a study of the policies of British and (principally) Australian legislators in the twentieth century, see Atkinson (2007).

[20] In the 1930s, the economists Plant (1934, pp. 167–195) and Coase (1937, pp. 386–495) prepared the ground for detailed examination of the social costs of copyright regulation. From the 1960s onwards, the contribution of a series of economists, including Arrow (1962), created a corpus of analysis that created the basis for rigorous continuing investigation of the economics of copyright. Simultaneously, jurists and legal academics, including Breyer (1970, pp. 281–355), sceptically examined official assumptions about the benefits of copyright regulation.

that property *is* theft—the inverse proposition to the industries' demand that property be protected *from* theft—most denied moral, utilitarian or any kind of inalienable justification for the scope and duration of exclusive rights.

File-sharing disputes brought into focus the extent to which, in popular perception, copyright monopoly subtracted from consumer welfare.[21] Peer-to-peer users, in word and action, declared opposition to what they considered the industries' demand for super-profit. The industries, they said, could recover investment and enrich themselves in traditional markets, but in the boundless realms of the digital universe, prescription failed: consent governed transactions.

Above all, digital copying showed that property laws are social compacts, not distillations of universal morality. Dissolution of such compacts suggests the necessity to negotiate new ones, not punish those who, like file-sharers, withdraw consent. At the end of the new century's first decade, however, industries remained determined to forestall infringement by prosecuting file-sharers and others in courts. Legislators remained devoted to the idea that copyright law 'balances' competing interests, and the idea that property rights do not readily admit derogation.

References

Arrow K (1962) Economic welfare and the allocation of resources for invention. In: The rate and direction of inventive activity: economic and social factors. National Bureau of Economic Research, Cambridge, pp 609–626

Atkinson B (2007) The true history of copyright: the Australian experience 1905–2005. Sydney University Press, Sydney

Breyer S (1970) The uneasy case for copyright: a study of copyright in books, photocopies and computer programs. Harv Law Rev 84(2):281–355

Coase R (1937) The nature of the firm: origins, evolution and development. Economica 4(16):386–495

Plant A (1934) The economic aspects of copyright in books. Economica 1(2):167–195

Proudhon PJ (1840/1994) What is property? An inquiry into the principle of right and of government (ed. and trans: Kelley DR, Smith BG). Cambridge University Press, Cambridge

[21] Most critics conceded that to the extent that it protects against free-riding, enabling producers to recoup investment, copyright law performs a socially useful function, providing legal surety to producers who, in the absence of protection, might withdraw from the market. The important question concerned for how long protection should last. In most, if not all, cases of commercial production, recoupment must occur within a few years if the investment is to be financially feasible.

Chapter 11
Dominance of the United States and Rise of Digital Economy

11.1 Open Source

Enforcement of property rights, especially by corporations hostile to peer-to-peer communication, drew criticism that industries espoused policies inimical to information dissemination. Zealous enforcement of rights in the digital environment doubtless struck the many programmers who contributed to the development of the internet's architecture as grimly ironic, for their free-wheeling exchange of ideas and multifarious contributions to software solutions helped to stimulate the development of the US software industry.

When the US Copyright Act of 1976 recognized copyright in computer programs, the outline of an industry made up of companies competing for market share could already be observed. In the 1960s, however, when communities of academics and researchers carried out most software development, programmers exchanged information freely, unconstrained by perceived need to keep programming advances confidential. By 1976, the computer industry seemed ready to disavow the collaborative ethos of a generation of programmers.

Their reaction to exclusionary policies that delimited access to software code in turn helped to create the 'free software' movement.[1] The movement embraced the collaborative ethos of the early programmers, who freely exchanged ideas and shared information with like-minded individuals. That ethos also found expression in the complementary open source software movement founded (or named) in the late 1990s. Both free software and open source movements affirmed the principle that free access[2] to source code in software, allowing programmers to modify or

[1] The ethos of the free software movement significantly influenced the 'free culture' movement that began in the late 1990s, and also emphasized the necessity for regulation and practice to facilitate public access to culture and knowledge.

[2] Richard Stallman, who established the Free Software Foundation in 1985, famously defined 'free software' as '"free" as in "free speech" not as in "free beer"'. Free software, he said, is 'a matter of liberty, not price' (see http://www.gnu.org/philosophy/free-sw.html).

B. Atkinson and B. Fitzgerald, *A Short History of Copyright*,
DOI 10.1007/978-3-319-02075-4_11, © Springer International Publishing Switzerland 2014

adapt a program, and distribute copies of the modified program, encouraged freedom, collaboration and exchange, each a social benefit.[3]

The idea of freedom, or individual liberty, as social objects stymied rather than facilitated by expansion of copyright regulation, encouraged a trend in the internet era away from proprietary values and towards belief in the social (and economic) utility of enabling people to freely collaborate in the production of works and their dissemination. The *Wikimedia* and *Creative Commons* organizations, the latter establishing standard licences for freely disseminating copyright works, were avatars of changed attitudes.[4]

11.2 The *Sony* Case

As the experts of WIPO and UNESCO, and courts and legislatures, adumbrated the scope of exclusive rights in ways that would eventually provoke into activism defenders of free culture and the public commons of information, the doctrines of fair dealing and fair use became the primary defence of alleged copyright infringers. This fact hinted at the doubtful accuracy of the principle that copyright law balances the interests of producers and users, since a string of court cases would show that concepts of fair use or fair dealing could not reliably be stretched to protect a range of activities that the ordinary person might be surprised to discover amounted to copyright infringement.

In the United States, perhaps the most famous modern case on fair use[5] began a continuing controversy, acted out periodically in courts, over the scope of permissible copying. In *Sony Corporation of America* v. *Universal City Studios* (1984),[6]

[3] Richard Stallman stated four freedoms promulgated by the free software movement (set out on FSF website www.gnu.org 'The Free Software Definition'): 'The freedom to run the program, for any purpose (freedom 0); The freedom to study how the program works, and change it to make it do what you wish (freedom 1). Access to the source code is a precondition for this; The freedom to redistribute copies so you can help your neighbor (freedom 2); The freedom to distribute copies of your modified versions to others (freedom 3). By doing this you can give the whole community a chance to benefit from your changes. Access to the source code is a precondition for this.'

[4] The Wikimedia Foundation (created 2003) operates various online wiki projects including Wikipedia and Wikemedia Commons. Creative Commons (founded 2002) makes available from websites catering to multiple jurisdictions six licence types: attribution, attribution-share-alike, attribution-no-derivatives, attribution-non-commercial, attribution-non-commercial-share-alike, attribution-non-commercial-no-derivatives. The Wikimedia Foundation and Creative Commons organizations accept the necessity for copyright regulation but criticize the exclusionary or proscriptive character of the law as applied to digital copying and communication. Both try to facilitate public access to information by supplying creators and collaborators with tools to disseminate and share works.

[5] The 1976 Copyright Act contained a fair use provision, followed by a library copying provision: 17 USC ss 107 and 108.

[6] 464 US 417 (1984).

the US Supreme Court, by a five to four majority, characterized as fair use private copying of television programmes on video cassettes.

The author of the majority decision, Justice Stevens, wrote that if a device like Sony's betamax video recorder was 'capable of substantial non-infringing uses' its manufacturer could not be held liable for negligence contributing to infringement. Consumers who used betamax recorders to 'time shift', to record programmes for later viewing, did so mostly for private non-commercial purposes. Time-shifting, said Justice Stevens, fell squarely within the boundaries of fair use.[7]

Despite lobbying from representatives of the movie industry, politicians, aware of the public mood on the subject of home copying, declined to overturn the result in the *Sony* case. They did nothing directly, though, to affirm it. Ironically, sales of betamax recorders, and VHS recorders (which vastly outsold Sony's product), created the video rental industry, which enormously increased the revenues of movie companies, without destroying box office sales, as widely predicted, most famously by Jack Valenti, President of the Motion Picture Association of America, who in 1982 declared: 'I say to you that the VCR is to the American film producer and the American public as the Boston strangler is to the woman home alone.'[8]

11.3 The Primacy of the United States

Supreme Court judgments, like that in *Sony*, mattered increasingly to the copyright world because from the 1960s onwards, the policy of US legislature, judiciary and government shaped the politics of international copyright and strongly influenced the decisions of politicians and judges in jurisdictions around the world. The reason for US predominance was, and remains, the economic power of its copyright industries.[9]

By the 1970s, numerous countries had replaced longstanding copyright statutes with new legislation that mostly united the fundamental elements of copyright

[7] Justice Blackmun's judgment for the minority found the scope of the Copyright Act's copying prohibition to be clear. The Act prohibited the making of a single unauthorized copy for personal or private use. Such copying might be fair use under the Act, and thus non-infringing, but fair use involved 'productive' use benefitting the public (hence fair use categories such as reporting or research). Blackmun asserted the legislature's 'desire to prevent the sale of products that are used almost exclusively to infringe copyrights'.

[8] Jack Valenti, testimony to the House Committee on the Judiciary Hearings on Home Recording of Copyrighted Works, 12 April 1982.

[9] Annual national trade statistics showed huge growth in the output of US copyright in the three decades following the passage of the 1976 Copyright Act. In 2005, the US copyright industries, the movie, television, software, publishing and music industries, contributed nearly US$820 billion to national GDP. In the same year, the copyright industries recorded foreign sales of over US$110 billion, ahead of nearly all other industrial sectors, including aeronautics, pharmaceuticals, agriculture and manufacturing.

protection enunciated by the Berne Convention or UCC and the tenets of neighbouring rights.

Reforms fostered belief in the social importance of proprietary rights, and industries asserted rights aggressively wherever they were infringed. The year that Congress passed the new US Copyright Act, 1976, is the watershed year of copyright reform.[10] The legislation created for the US entertainment and software industries an unshakeable foundation of legal surety on which they relied to press claims for market preferment or domination in foreign jurisdictions.

The Act of 1976 recognized copyright in computer programs and introduced the schema of protection familiar to signatories of the Berne and Rome Conventions.[11] Legislative recognition of copyright in computer programs, in particular, gave impetus to the emergence of something resembling an American imperium in the copyright world. In the quarter century following enactment, as the entertainment industries asserted copyright around the globe, computer programming utilizing digital electronics transformed the world.[12]

The primacy of Silicon Valley is only one part of the story of what made the United States the great source of economic, technical and creative energies that transformed the world's communications infrastructure and accelerated the digital revolution, the effects of which are felt in most aspects of social and economic life. The digital revolution involved change to the means of communication, and invention of new modes of communication, and its transfigurative power manifested in what technology now permitted: instantaneous transmission and exchange of information, and its replication.

The digital revolution is thus an information revolution, and the US software industry its epicentre. Software, like no other technology or product, symbolized American transcendence. The extraordinary creative leaps of the US software industry, which made possible simultaneous engineering innovations and the great leap forward in digital communications technology, inspired in the interested population of the world an overriding reaction of awe.[13]

---

[10] The new legislation replaced a statute nearly 70 years old, one passed by Congress a year before Mark Twain's death and a decade after the end of a century in which US publishers were stigmatized as unconscionable pirates of foreign works. The US in 1976 manifested very different attitudes to copyright protection. The most obvious difference could be seen in reactions to piracy. Increasingly, after 1976 the US appeared to observers as the implacable enemy of copyright piracy wherever it could be found.

[11] The US remained outside the Berne family and would not become a convention signatory until 1989.

[12] Australia protected computer programs as literary works in 1984 and Britain in 1985, and in the same year Japan, the Federal Republic of Germany and France followed suit.

[13] More exactly than any other synthesis of creative design and industrial innovation, software products illustrated Arthur C. Clarke's third law, that '[a]ny sufficiently advanced technology is indistinguishable from magic' (1984, pp. 29 and 36).

11.4 US Copyright Trade Policy

The burst of activity that produced a new US copyright statute presaged a larger dynamism, expressed in an efflorescence of American power in international trade politics. In a relatively short period, from the beginning of the Uruguay Round of GATT trade talks in 1987, to the formation of the World Trade Organization in 1994, and the signing of WIPO's Copyright Treaty in 1996,[14] the United States inspired the transformation of international copyright law.

The march of US power, directed by the magnates of copyright industries, resulted in reformation of the administration and content of international copyright law. The changes greatly increased the economic leverage of those industries, and owed everything to the collaboration of industries and US government. The importuning of industry leaders in the office suites of Capitol Hill and, above all, in the Office of the United States Trade Representative (USTR), created an energy that radiated through the world's copyright decision-making bodies and the world's legislatures.

The genesis of the USTR's copyright trade policy is discernible in the beginnings of industry-government cooperation in the 1970s. In that decade, many US policy-makers were demoralized by flooding Japanese imports, inflation and the rising evidence of US economic decline. The seemingly unstoppable growth of the Japanese electronics and computer manufacturing industries suggested to some Americans that their country would soon be supplanted as the world's leading producer of sophisticated technology.

Apparent decline, however, masked the beginnings of metamorphosis. The US remained, at the end of the 1970s, by far the world's dominant economic power. Regulatory reforms designed to liberalize the financial system, and facilitate creation of the so-called knowledge economy, gradually reawakened Americans to the power of their economy.

In the 1980s, the US government listened with friendly ears to demands for a strategy for rights enforcement in foreign jurisdictions. In 1984, the formation of the International Intellectual Property Alliance created an insistent new voice that has been heard regularly since in the offices of Capitol Hill and the USTR.[15]

Internationally, the US pressed for international agreement on stringent, enforceable intellectual property standards, negotiated bilateral agreements to fill lacunae in protection and rigorously policed international compliance with IP standards. In the 1980s, the USTR began, on behalf of copyright industries, to aggressively

[14] Also the WIPO Performances and Phonograms Treaty adopted by WIPO states 20 December 1996.

[15] The Australian scholars John Braithwaite and Peter Drahos have published a number of works on the alignment of IP objectives with US trade policy. See, for example, Braithwaite and Drahos (2000, 2002).

police compliance of different countries with US-prescribed standards of IP protection.[16]

US IP trade policy planning played a role in the formation of the WTO in 1994. The WTO's General Council oversees three subsidiary councils, one of which is responsible for TRIPS, and also supervises dispute resolution. Under the rubric of TRIPS, the USTR monitors international compliance with intellectual property standards, and threatens delinquent nations with sanctions under Special 301 or action under the WTO's dispute settlement procedures.[17]

11.5 Code and Digital Communication

The rise of the software industry and spread of computers soon resulted in development of digital networks, which allowed for communication between computers. The local benefits of network connection spurred programmers to attempt global interconnection, and from their efforts came the internet, the agglomeration of millions of network links transmitting information using standard protocols (the Internet Protocol Suite or TCP/IP), as seemingly boundless as the cosmos.

Digital communication via the internet—which began rapidly to connect computers across the world from the middle of the 1990s—dematerialized the process of reproduction and distribution regulated by copyright law. Once digitized, copyright works formerly supplied in material form—such as books, CDs and DVDs—could be copied and distributed, or shared, by millions, or hundreds of millions, of computer users.

[16] Trade concessions available to designated developing countries were revoked if they did not effectively curtail piracy and counterfeiting. The Special 301 Watch List, introduced in 1988, continues to provide a running log of nations under USTR surveillance for alleged failure to implement regulatory or enforcement obligations. The US threatens, and can impose, trade sanctions for deemed non-compliance under Special 301. The Watchlist was created under section 301 of the 1974 US Trade Act.

[17] The US also undertook, especially from the late 1990s, a highly effective programme of concluding bilateral copyright agreements with both developed nations and less developed nations, in order to secure recognition of the rights of US copyright holders and enforcement of their rights in foreign jurisdictions. US Free Trade Agreements have proved particularly effective in securing US IP/trade goals, linking acceptance of rigorous IPR (and its enforcement) with the grant of US trade concessions considered desirable by the contracting nation. Such agreements are sometimes known as 'TRIPS plus', since they impose the obligation to comply with the TRIPS Agreement, with special requirements additional to TRIPS obligations—such as the obligation to enact measures prohibiting the use of circumvention devices to interfere with digital rights management (DRM) measures, to institute extensive criminal sanctions for certain offences or extend the term of copyright consistent with US legislative changes (20-year term extensions for different copyrights). See further the proposed *Anti-Counterfeiting Trade Agreement* (ACTA), negotiated by over 30 countries led by the US and the EC. ACTA creates enforcement standards that considerably exceed in scope the minimum standards in the TRIPS Agreement and is intended to facilitate international suppression of trade in counterfeit and pirate copies of IP products.

In 2012, over 2.405 billion people used the internet.[18] Users across the globe copying, disseminating or sharing information testified to the interconnectedness of the internet. Its advocates perceived in its pervasiveness and utility sources of human freedom and advancement, and no one denied its extraordinary potential to transform modes of commerce and enterprise.

The transformative potential of the internet delighted those who looked forward to a future in which the low cost of copying and dissemination would cause the price charged for access to online copyright material to fall steeply.[19] Copyright industries, feeling their way in a new and, so they felt, lawless universe were less delighted. They felt beleaguered, and alarmed by the growing evidence that in cyberspace an ever-growing alliance of internet users rejected the legal parameters of the earthbound material world, repudiating monopolies and rules that in the twentieth century allowed the industries to grow rich.

In practice, the internet acutely demonstrated its power to test the premises of long-standing regulation. For example, copyright law, according to its defenders, balanced the interests of producers and consumers of copyright material. They argued that copyright monopolies encouraged productive output. Their absence would encourage piracy and thus discourage production.

Now, the ways in which internet users communicated and downloaded copyright material cast doubt on these staple justifications of copyright law. Online copyright piracy proliferated, yet the industries most affected, the music and movie businesses, despite predictions of catastrophe, to some extent adapted production and distribution processes, and, in any event, continued to flourish.[20] Productive incentive did not seem to diminish.

Some argued that, unobserved, manipulation of digital technology could transform the internet into an information dystopia. Professor Lawrence Lessig, one of the originators of the study of cyberspace law, declared in a seminal book that software, creating internet architecture, determined in practice internet user rights. Software code outstripped legal code in regulatory effect. Those who designed code created means to control the supply of information.[21]

---

[18] Internet Usage Statistics at 30 June 2012, compiled by Internet World Stats at www.internetworldstats.com/stats.htm.

[19] That the marginal cost of digital reproduction and dissemination on the internet is zero or near zero is considered uncontroversial. The cost of production and dissemination for producers is of course greater than zero and includes investment and enforcement costs. The technology cost involved in digital copying and dissemination is, however, as low for producers as for individual internet users.

[20] According to the Recording Industry of America Consumer Profile 2008 (http://www.riaa.com/keystatistics.php?content_selector=consumertrends), the value of sales of recorded music fell by half in the 9 years after 1999. Although not compensating for the fall, sales from music-streaming services provided an increasing source of revenue, and licensing arrangements (including contracts with YouTube and cell phone companies such as Nokia), concert ticketing, associated merchandising, advertising, sponsorship and festival and events sales generated growing revenues. 'IFPI's *Digital Music Report* for 2013 stated that 'the global recorded music industry is on a path to recovery, fuelled by licensed music services and rapid expansion into new markets internationally.'

[21] Lessig (1999).

History shows that the use of any code to assert control is not proof against reaction. In the case of the internet, encryption does not forestall decryption. In the decade after Professor Lessig published his thesis, software and legal code followed similar paths of proscription, but programmers and hackers defied code limitations.

The politics of copyright in the twenty-first century, although ostensibly concerned with questions of codes, followed a pattern recognizable in the history of copyright law-making. Through prohibitions, industries asserted the applicability of proprietary rights in cyberspace and immediately encountered broad resistance, with critics declaring outrageously presumptuous claims to control the whole nebula of the internet.

References

Braithwaite J, Drahos P (2000) Global business regulation. Cambridge University Press, Cambridge

Braithwaite J, Drahos P (2002) Information feudalism: who owns the knowledge economy? Earthscan, London

Clarke AC (1984) Profiles of the future: an inquiry into the limits of the possible. Holt, Rinehart and Winston, New York

Lessig L (1999) Code and other laws of cyberspace. Basic Books, New York

Chapter 12
Dissent and P2P

12.1 Internet Dissent

In the past, copyright regulation rarely caused public controversy, since industries and governments worked together to create laws that seemed to most citizens remote from daily experience. Now, however, the public knew very well that new laws prohibited most unauthorized dealings in copyright material on the internet. Many regarded regulation as the harbinger of political or commercial oppression, and others who accepted the necessity for code agreed that new copyright laws were inimical to information dissemination and exchange.

The argument over internet copyright laws, and the practices they regulate, thus became a political argument over the merits of proprietary restriction and the limits of individual freedom. The debate placed the copyright industries, for the first time in their histories, at a polemical disadvantage, for every user of the internet could see the opportunities for communication and exchange of information supplied via the internet. How could industries apply earthly laws to this virtual macrocosm? Who could claim to rule in this deep space?

The seeming limitlessness of the internet did not preclude communication. Software made its vast spaces instantly traversable, and internet users, staring into screens and travelling across realms, could feel the excitement of exploration, the joy of unconstraint, the thrill of conversation untrammelled.

Many felt angry that into this world of freedom and opportunity industries intruded with mercenary demands. They reacted by refusing to pay fees-for-use demanded by copyright owners and, in many instances, with informed dissent. The internet dissenters subjected the premises of copyright law, and the presumptions of industries and policy-makers—long taken for granted in terrestrial jurisdictions—to sustained attack. The battle over payment-for-use was, and is, broad ranging, and focused, for the first decade of the twenty-first century, on the prolific practice of internet users swapping, or sharing, digital musical files.

B. Atkinson and B. Fitzgerald, *A Short History of Copyright*,
DOI 10.1007/978-3-319-02075-4_12, © Springer International Publishing Switzerland 2014

The music industry, supported by legal code, attacked file-sharing practices, repeating the hackneyed phrase that unauthorized copying is property theft. But, in cypberspace, beyond the terrestrial realms in which legal code is readily enforceable, it found itself at a disadvantage.

The difficulty of policing illegal internet activity, such as file-sharing, resulted principally from the numbers of users engaging in activity—ranging from millions, to tens of millions—and their geographic dispersion. Law enforcers faced the second difficulty of resentment. A sense of injustice at the content of legal code and the enforcement activities of industries seen as profiteers fuelled the anger of millions of internet users and encouraged dissent that began to undermine the legitimacy of copyright laws.

12.2 Napster

The appearance in 1999 of the file-sharing service Napster announced the beginning of the file-sharing or peer-to-peer (P2P) phenomenon. Users relied on the indexing system on Napster's central server to identify copies of recorded music available, in compressed MP3 format, for downloading from the machines of other users. In Napster's approximately 18-month span of activity, downloads totalled in the billions.[1]

The Recording Industry Association of America (RIAA) wasted no time in calling Napster a pirate organization profiting from distribution of unauthorized copies of recorded music. District and federal courts accepted prima facie the RIAA's contention that Napster's activities infringed copyright,[2] although the latter found that its file-sharing system permitted substantial non-infringing uses.

According to the courts, Napster knew or had reason to know of the infringing activity and had avoided policing infringement in order to increase the number of users and thus expand the audience available to future advertisers. The federal court found Napster likely to have committed contributory and vicarious copyright infringement.[3] The *Sony* defence was held not to be applicable. It was overridden where there was actual knowledge (contributory liability) and could not be asserted as a defence in a claim for vicarious liability.

---

[1] The peak of downloads came in February 2001: P2P users used Napster to download 2.7 billion audio files. See (among other sources) Talab (2002), pp. 3–6.

[2] The RIAA alleged direct, contributory and vicarious copyright infringement. ***A&M Records, Inc. et al.* v. *Napster*** (No C 99-5183 MHP No C 00-0074 MHP 2000), USDC Northern California; *A&M Records, Inc.* v. *Napster, Inc.*, 239 F3d 1004 (*Ninth Circuit* 2001).

[3] With liability to be determined at trial.

Napster defended the RIAA's suit[4] on a number of grounds.[5] According to the appeals court, file-sharers engaged in infringing copying of creative material. They were not, as Napster asserted, protected by the fair use doctrine based on 'space-shifting' or copying a purchased work in a different format.

As modified at the direction of the higher court, the district court injunction issued against Napster proved devastating. Required to prevent access to files notified as infringing and unable to satisfy the court of its capacity or willingness to prevent illegal file-sharing, Napster ceased operations in 2001 and filed for bankruptcy the following year.

12.3 Attitudes of Industries and Courts

Beginning with the Napster hearings, the P2P wars brought to public attention the extraordinary opportunities for communication offered by digital networks, as well as the enthusiasm of young people for new modes of information exchange made possible by the internet. That enthusiasm foreshadowed the emergence of social-networking sites, such as Facebook, and video-sharing sites, such as YouTube.

Young people wrote the software for each of these sites but, more relevantly, digital networks, and the constructive possibilities of software programming, enabled them, with minimal capital, to create the means for untold numbers of internet users to enter cyberspace for social purposes. The courts, however, tended to regard the social aspects of the internet with suspicion. The copyright industries, which might have been expected to embrace opportunities for online commerce, seemingly saw the internet as a lawless realm that must be subdued and regulated, then exploited.

The industries reacted predictably, in the manner of property owners throughout history, alarmed by destabilization of accepted norms of control. They could not see that digital networks, and allied modalities for distributing information, offered possibilities for creating markets of willing consumers. As before, ideas of consumer sovereignty and adaptation to novel consumer needs seemed beyond

[4] The RIAA sought in the district court, and obtained, a preliminary injunction preventing Napster from permitting file-sharing of music copyright to RIAA members. However the federal court promptly stayed the order pending appeal.

[5] These were as follows: fair use permits alleged copying applicability of *Audio Home Recording Act* to computers; the operation of the *Sony* defence; Napster protected by the safe harbor provisions of the *Digital Millennium Copyright Act* (DMCA); waiver of copyright; implied licence; and copyright misuse. The ninth ciruit appeals court rejected these grounds with the exception of the DMCA safe harbor provisions. The court stated that sufficient doubt had been raised concerning the application of the safe harbor provisions to Napster to sustain the interim relief sought.

comprehension. Fear of reduction—of proprietary rights or of the returns guaranteed by those rights—dominated thinking.

It is the reaction of the judiciary, however, that caused the most concern to those who saw P2P and social networks as the harbinger of a new age welcoming to information exchange and the liberal benefits of dissemination. If code is law, courts appeared willing to interpret law to restrict, rather than enlarge, the free flow of information.[6]

In this respect, they too were predictable: the law historically upholds proprietary rights, against reason, common sense or revolution. With a few exceptions, throughout the history of copyright the courts have sided with the forces of restriction and enclosure. In Napster, the courts did not deviate from this trend.

Eighteen copyright law professors filed in the appeals court an amicus curiae brief, in which they pointed to the danger of concluding that the effect of a particular application of technology—in this case the effect of unauthorized copying on sales—is reason to outlaw the technology.[7] Their arguments found little favour.

In *Sony*, 16 years before, the Supreme Court, by a five to four majority, followed the lead of Justice Stevens and rejected the idea that because technology potentially undermines property rights it must be prohibited. Had the court then chosen instead to follow the minority leader Justice Blackmun, it would, in the clearest terms, have favoured monopoly rights, a source of economic inefficiency and social disadvantage, over innovation, a source of dynamism and social opportunity.[8]

In Napster, the amicus brief of law professors explained that while the type of distribution involved in file-sharing challenged the recording industry's method of controlling distribution through approved outlets, the purpose of copyright law was not 'to protect existing business models'.[9] The courts, however, as a succession of file-sharing cases showed, were concerned to protect the economic welfare of the recording and movie industries.

---

[6] As, for example, in the case of *Warner Bros and J.K. Rowling* v. *RDR Books* 575 FSupp 2d 513 (2008). The defendant published an encyclopedia, the *Harry Potter Lexicon*, a guide to the world of Harry Potter, that quoted portions of the Harry Potter books without attribution. The US district court granted the author J.K. Rowling an injunction restraining publication. The defence of fair use failed because the borrowings were substantial, albeit that the encyclopedia was a reference work.

[7] Amended Brief Amicus Curiae of Copyright Law Professors in Support of Reversal, Consortium of 18 Copyright Law Professors, *Napster Inc.* v. *A&M Records et al.* (2000).

[8] Justice Blackmun's judgment for the minority interpreted statutory fair use provisions to exclude copying for personal or private use. He asserted the legislature's 'desire to prevent the sale of products that are used almost exclusively to infringe copyrights'.

[9] Amended Brief Amicus Curiae of Copyright Law Professors in Support of Reversal, Consortium of 18 Copyright Law Professors, *Napster Inc.* v. *A&M Records et al.* (2000) at 4.

12.4 Changes in P2P Software

Napster's software enabled file-sharers to identify MP3 files for downloading by reference to a central server. The service could thus be said to be offered directly by Napster, and the courts determined that Napster could prevent copyright infringement by removing information about infringing files or connection to them. Additionally, the courts determined that infringement facilitated by Napster's service caused consumers to download music illegally in preference to purchasing compact discs.

The next generation of file-sharing services offered by a range of providers tried, with varying degrees of success, to avoid infringement liability by decentralizing methods of distribution and permitted sharing of movie or video files as well as audio files. Kazaa and Grokster offered software that enabled users to download files directly from identifying computers, without using indexes generated on a central server. Unlike Napster, the services made profits, attracting advertisers who could deliver their messages in embedded adware and spyware.

Gnutella, a P2P protocol utilizing open source software enabled a multiplying list of 'clients' to write free or proprietary applications that offered internet users a choice of ways to use the Gnutella network. Gnutella is an open protocol used by popular clients such as LimeWire,[10] Morpheus, XoloX and BearShare, and functions autonomously—that is, network access is not mediated by a central server.

The BitTorrent protocol, first released in 2001, created a new form of autonomous P2P communication. BitTorrent disaggregated large files in segments downloaded and shared by peers, who reconstitute files by exchanging copies of downloaded segments. Together, Gnutella and BitTorrent accounted for about half of all P2P traffic in 2009 (see Hamilton 2009).[11] By 2013, uTorrent dominated the market, followed at a distance by BitTorrent.

12.5 Grokster

The entertainment industries, alarmed at extraordinary volumes of illegally copied copyright material distributed by internet users, found the US Supreme Court receptive to their message that P2P software posed a radical threat to copyrights.

---

[10] See *Arista Records LLC* v. *LimeWire LLC* 2010 WL 1914816 (S.D.N.Y. May 11, 2010) which found LimeWire liable for copyright infringement on the primary ground of inducement, the doctrine enunciated in the *MGM Grand* v. *Groskter* case (USC 2005)—discussed below. LimeWire was aware of substantial infringement by users, made efforts to attract infringing users, enabled and assisted infringement, depended on infringing activities for commercial viability and did not take mitigation action.

[11] TorrentFreak.com stated in 2009 that BitTorrent's share was well over 40 %. In 2013 OPSWAT's *Market Share Report* on P2P recorded uTorrent's market share as 54.5 % and BitTorrent's share (in second place) as 7.4 %

They launched proceedings against Grokster, and in 2005 the Supreme Court halted the service (and that of Kazaa) in *MGM Studios Inc.* v. *Grokster Ltd.*[12] The Court stressed that demonstrated intent to induce infringement, shown by clear expression or taking other affirmative steps, amounted to infringement.

Evidence of Grokster's intent to induce could be found in its clear intention to offer a service that replaced Napster, its unwillingness to provide filters to limit unlawful copying and the company's profiting from advertising sales. Judged by the standard enunciated in the case, file-sharing services dedicated to profit, and undiscriminating about the legality of P2P activities, would be liable for copyright infringement and thus subject to closure.

Members of the Court looked closely at the 'substantial non-infringing uses' test in *Sony* and split evenly on the question whether the *Sony* precedent could be adduced in the defendant's favour. Justice Ginsburg, joined by Chief Justice Rehnquist and Justice Kennedy, distinguished between Grokster users, the great bulk of whom (according to their Honours) infringed copyright, and the users of Sony betamax recorders. A substantial proportion of the latter group, according to the Court's majority judgment in 1984, engaged in time-shifting for private, non-commercial purposes—a non-infringing use. *Grokster* uses 'were ... overwhelmingly' infringing and 'this infringement was the overwhelming source of revenue from the products'.[13] Weighed against these facts, evidence of non-infringing use did not preclude a finding of infringement against Grokster.

Justice Breyer, joined by Justices O'Connor and Stevens, adopted the opposite position. The *Sony* test provided that if a copying device were capable of substantial non-infringing uses, it could not be judged to be infringing. While non-infringing uses 'account for only a small percentage of total number of uses of Grokster's product' they were still 'substantial' if judged by the standard of assessment applied in *Sony*.[14]

Of the two concurrences, it might be said that written by Breyer focused more objectively on the function of technology. Ginsburg's judgment focused more subjectively on purpose of use. The Ginsburg concurrence suggested that on the question of fair use, half of the members of the nation's highest court seem preoccupied by moral concern to deter piracy, rather than analysis of the purpose and effect of allegedly infringing technology.

Division over *Sony* did not mask the truth that suppliers of P2P software must now tread on eggshells to avoid legal attack. The test of inducement, involving consideration of intent, unlawful purpose and steps taken to encourage infringement, might in future be applied to prohibit conduct identical in principle to that of Sony selling video recorders in the early 1980s. If the object of the doctrine is to prevent piracy, it inevitably censures P2P communication, the object of which is unmediated exchange of information, and must include unauthorized copying.

---

[12] 545 US 913 (2005).

[13] Concurring opinion by Ruth Bader Ginsburg.

[14] Concurring opinion of Stephen Breyer.

Such activity inevitably involves, on a large scale or small, unauthorized exchange of copyright information. The difference in principle between the *Sony* and *Grokster* decisions is philosophical, reflecting judicial attitude to control. The Supreme Court's majority in 1984 refused to stymie innovation and abrogate consumer sovereignty by, in effect, outlawing recorders. In 2005, the Court recognized no such restraint on the industry's power to control development and dissemination of new technology.

To critics of illegal file-sharing, P2P networks simulated the Hobbesian state of nature dreaded by property advocates. They encouraged, said their critics, predatory, vicious, behaviour. Even after Grokster, they were ungoverned and possibly ungovernable, and the task of suppressing illegal downloading could be likened to swatting fleas.

12.6 Politics and Enforcement

Staring at bedlam, or so they declared, copyright industries redoubled their efforts to regulate behaviour by changing code. They utilized watermarking and digital rights management applications to prevent illegal copying of digital products and lobbied law-makers to further criminalize the varieties of infringing behaviour.

If code is law, politics is law-in-waiting, and the crucible in which proprietary claims harden into irreducible principles, adding more volume, complexity and proscription to legal rules. In the United States, politics delivered to industries the advantages of favourable laws and the right to use software code, as best it might, to restrict infringement. The internet's digital arteries, however, pulsated unconscious of code prescriptions.

Networks were so numerous, and complex, that code enforcers could identify only a minority of those who trafficked or downloaded copyright material in breach of code. High points of legislative gain for copyright industries, the *Digital Millennium Copyright Act* (DMCA) and the *Copyright Term Extension Act* (CTEA) of 1998,[15] asserted proprietary rights to an unruly audience of users alienated by the claims of property—and often heedless of its sanctions. Like twin Cerberuses, planted to guard the gates of the internet, the CTEA, and DCMA bared fangs at anyone who threatened copyright owners' control over the variety of digital uses.

Among other things, the DMCA amended US copyright law to prohibit the circumvention of a technological measure that effectively controlled access to a copyright work and the manufacture, supply or sale of a device or service that

[15] The DMCA introduced provisions concerning circumvention of technological protection measures and 'safe harbors'. To qualify for safe harbor protection, ISPs must adopt and implement termination policies and accommodate copyright owners' protection measures. ISPs are not required to monitor or access in violation of other laws. The CTEA (or Sonny Bono Act) extended copyright terms for authors by 20 years. For copyright authors the term increased to life plus 70 years.

enabled a user to circumvent technological measures in the form of an access or copy control. These provisions, implementing the WIPO copyright treaties, were replicated around the world. A point of great contention concerned the grounds upon which circumvention or the supply and use of a circumvention device was legally justified.

The CTEA's extension of copyright terms by 20 years (which resulted in extension of protection for authors to life plus 70 years) came under review in 2003 in *Eldred* v. *Ashcroft*.[16] Eric Eldred, who created an online library of public domain works accessible to the public, challenged in the Washington federal district court the constitutionality of the CTEA. Surprisingly, after negative reception of the case by first instance and appeals judges, the case proceeded to the Supreme Court.

Eldred, joined by other publishers, and amici, was opposed by the Attorney General Ashcroft, and amici.[17] He argued that the constitutional copyright clause and the first amendment guaranteeing free speech jointly precluded continuing extensions beyond a natural limit implied in the constitutional clause.[18] Unpersuaded, the Supreme Court delivered a seven to two judgment against Eldred.

The majority judgment, written by Justice Ginsburg, found that the constitution did not forbid continued extension. Provided that Congress did not enact a perpetual term, it could legitimately legislate increases to the duration of copyright. Justice Breyer, dissenting, pointed out that extensions made the copyright term, in effect, perpetual. Even if the incentive to create works derived from expectation of reward, an author could not plausibly be said to be motivated to reward distant descendants, such as great-grandchildren.

Justice Stevens, also dissenting, observed that exclusive emphasis on rewarding creators could distort markets. While the much shorter patent term supposedly encouraged continued innovation by allowing a monopoly term to recoup investment, the necessity for a lengthy copyright term, given the less quantifiable nature of the author's investment, was far less obvious.

12.7 Safe Harbors and Third Party Liability

The DMCA included a provision, section 512, to protect a new entrant to copyright politics, the internet service provider, or ISP. This provision, providing ISP 'safe harbours', became an early focus of the *Napster* case, when Napster unsuccessfully

---

[16] 573 US 186.

[17] Though Solicitor General Olson delivered government arguments.

[18] Professor Lawrence Lessig, counsel for Eldred, based his strategy on the presumption that the Court, having in recent years rejected government arguments for unlimited legislative power in relation to matters relating to commerce—and contrawise affirmed limits to the legislature's power under the constitutional commerce clause—would recognize in the constitutional progress clause inherent limitation on Congress's power to extend the copyright term.

claimed ISP status. It increased the segregation of copyright politics, protecting from contributory liability the corporate entities that the film and music industries identified as more capable of policing illegal downloading.

The safe harbor provision appeared to contradict the claim that ISPs ought, on behalf of copyright holders, to regulate P2P activity, but the doctrine of inducement gave impetus to industries arguing that ISPs ought not to escape secondary liability for the illegal activities of subscribers. Debate turned on the question of *control*: copyright industries argued that ISPs, controlling access to technology and records of subscriber activity, could more effectively police infringements, and assist in enforcement.

The battle of ISPs and copyright industries over secondary liability remains intense. ISPs deny that control over access urges a derivative obligation to monitor and, where necessary, prohibit user activity. In member nations, the balance of political favour may be tilting slightly in favour of the music and recording industries. In 2009, France's National Assembly, after abandoning proposals for ISP-levied copyright use fees, enacted a 'Three Strikes' law aimed at punishing illegal P2P activity.[19]

In Australia, the balance shifted in favour of ISPs in a case brought by US (and Australian) entertainment companies to try to establish a strict standard of ISP liability for third party copyright infringements. In November 2008, a group of Hollywood film studios and others[20] filed suit in the federal court, alleging that by not warning infringing users over infringements notified and then cancelling internet connections of continuing offenders iiNet, Australia's third largest ISP, authorized infringements.

In *Roadshow Films Pty Ltd* v. *iiNet Limited (No 3)*,[21] the Australian Federation Against Copyright Theft, representing the film studios, asserted that over 59 weeks, iiNet subscribers, using BitTorrent software, made available for illegal downloading nearly 100,000 unauthorized copies of copyright films. AFACT, through an agent, monitored internet usage. Over the relevant period, AFACT regularly notified iiNet of alleged repeat infringements by iiNet subscribers. According to AFACT, iiNet refused to cancel their contracts.

---

[19] *Loi Favorisant la diffusion et la protection de la creation sur Internet* (Law in support of the diffusion and protection of creative works on the internet) or, informally, the HADOPI Law. The law allows HADOPI, or the 'High Authority for Copyright Protection and Dissemination of Works on the Internet', to monitor internet activity and instruct suspected copyright infringers to cease the infringing activity—first by email and then by registered delivery post. If warnings are ignored HADOPI is empowered to pass the matter to a magistrate who can order that the offender's internet access be discontinued and impose heavy fines and a prison sentence. The law in its original form was declared unconstitutional by France's constitutional court because it permitted HADOPI, not a magistrate, to order internet disconnection. This defect was cured in new legislation passed in August 2009.

[20] Including Universal Pictures, Paramount Pictures, Warner Bros, Sony Pictures Entertainment, 20th Century Fox and Disney.

[21] [2010] FCA 24.

Justice Cowdroy agreed with iiNet's counsel that the burden of policing copyright infringement and enforcing rights lies with copyright proprietors. The ISP could not be said to authorize infringements by subscribers using BitTorrent, since 'iiNet has no control over the BitTorrent system and is not responsible for the operation of the BitTorrent system'.[22] Nor did iiNet in any way endorse or encourage infringement.[23] Crucially, iiNet did not supply, or authorize supply of, the 'means' of infringement.[24] Thus the pendulum of influence swung, however briefly, away from copyright industries.[25]

References

Hamilton M (2009) Taking a look at P2P: Gnutella and BitTorrent. breakingpointsystems.com/community/blog. 27 July 2009

Talab RS (2002) Napster, distributed peer sharing and its chronology: "you say you want a revolution?". TechTrends 46(3):3–6

[22] The term 'authorize' is used in different jurisdictions in different ways, and its use may cause some confusion to readers of judgments analysing secondary liability in copyright cases. See the discussion in the amicus brief in the 2005 *Grokster* case (*Brief of Amicus Curiae Sharman Networks Ltd in Support of Respondents*)—'the word "authorize" is used in one sense in the United States, in another very different sense in the international treaties and the EU, and in yet a third very different sense in the Commonwealth countries (wherein the term has yielded conflicting results at the highest judicial level)'.

[23] Evidence showed that iiNet's service suffered from bandwidth restrictions caused by illegal downloading.

[24] His Honour distinguished 'means' from 'a precondition to infringement occurring'—supply of internet access by an ISP does not supply 'means' to infringement by ISP subscribers but it is a 'precondition for online infringement' by ISP subscribers (*Roadshow Films Pty Ltd* v. *iiNet Limited* (*No 3*) [2010] FCA 24, judgment, Summary point 12).

[25] In February 2011, Australia's Full Federal Court, though on distinct grounds, upheld Justice Cowdroy's judgment 2:1 and dismissed the film studios' appeal: *Roadshow Films Pty Ltd v iiNet Ltd* [2011] FCAFC 23. In April 2012, the High Court unanimously dismissed Roadshow Films's appeal against the Full Federal Court's judgment *Roadshow Films Pty Ltd v iiNet Ltd* [2012] HCA 16.

Chapter 13
Access and Networking

13.1 Access

At the heart of the P2P or, more accurately, fair use battles lay two distinct conceptions of information regulation. Copyright law resulted from the desire of political authorities (be they absolute or, in varying shades, representative) and private interests (first publishers, then others) to control the supply of information for political or economic advantage. The law developed with little regard for the wishes of those interested in, having need of, seeking out or 'consuming' information, that group of people far greater in number than politicians or businesses—the public.

By degrees, mass application of communication technologies—record player, radio, television—created the idea of an information consumer and allowed that the public might be said to have needs and wants that could be identified and supplied. The public, however, communicated in the passive voice, its preferences articulated and interpreted by the industries that wanted to sell information and products.

The rise of the software industry, and the spread, across the world, of a digital revolution, changed everything. The passive voice of the public changed to an active voice. P2P software resulted from the efforts of programmers, sometimes motivated by profit, sometimes not, to create a means of unweighted communication—that is, free exchange of information unweighted by prices and other restrictions on use that copyright industries attached to information supply.

In the corporate sphere, the great access corporations that emerged as the internet grew—for example, Yahoo and Google—also transcended the limitations of price and conditionality that the copyright industries had long ago adopted, and which greatly hindered their capacity to adapt to the online world. The access corporations, like P2P hackers and developers, offered weightless information supply. Securing revenue from advertisers, they offered the public free access to information and, unlike the copyright industries, placed no limitation on access.

Music and film industries, staring into the internet's endless space, in which countless atoms of information pinged uncontrolled between users, choked and litigated. The access corporations, by contrast, welcomed the endlessness of

B. Atkinson and B. Fitzgerald, *A Short History of Copyright*,
DOI 10.1007/978-3-319-02075-4_13, © Springer International Publishing Switzerland 2014

cyberspace and sought to open more portals to infinity. Slowly, very slowly, politicians and industries opened their eyes to the public's insatiable liking for weightless information, though they continued to chart a reactionary pattern in legislation.

In a certain sense, the philosophical differences between those who sought to control information supply on the internet and those who sought its liberation were age old. The battle between forces insisting on control or repression and those demanding freedom or liberty is, in a simple way, the story of copyright itself. Ironically, many of those who battled for liberty became monopolists along the way.[1] In many ways, copyright law represents the triumph of the forces of control, those that appropriated proprietary powers to govern information supply for their own profit and gain.

The internet enables corporations like Google, still for profit and gain, to escape the model of proprietary control enforced by copyright law, because it overturns in practice a presumption integral to the theory and practice of copyright adherents since the days of the booksellers 300 years ago. This is the idea that unless carefully regulated or controlled, the supply of information will dwindle, since information is scarce, and its few producers unwilling to continue production unless protected by monopoly.[2]

13.2 Scarcity and Access

The concept of information scarcity, if accepted, inevitably leads legislatures to enact restrictive copyright laws. In the English-speaking world, helpfully for copyright monopolists, the idea of scarcity has dominated a great deal of political thinking and, from the time of John Locke, has underpinned justifications for proprietary rights.[3]

Locke argued that property arises from the admixture of nature and human labour, and government—laws—must protect property in order to ensure continued productive labour, and thus society removed from the state of nature.[4]

---

[1] In the seventeenth century in England, parliament fought against the absolute claims of the monarchy and the system of crown privileges or monopolies bestowed by the king on vested interest. However, early in the eighteenth century, parliament created in the Statute of Anne, new monopolies, ostensibly in favour of authors, actually for the benefit of publishers. Similarly, the American colonies rebelled against crown monopolies, and the United States declared itself in favour of free speech and dissemination of 'useful' copyright material for public benefit. However, Congress granted copyright holders proprietary monopolies of increasing length.

[2] It could be argued that access corporations are quasi-monopolies aiming for monopoly. However, a key difference with traditional copyright industries is that their primary functional aim is to facilitate information access.

[3] Locke (1689/1988).

[4] Note the so-called 'Lockean Proviso', the moral principle qualifying Locke's theory of property. The creation of property, wrote Locke, must not deprive others of the opportunity to benefit from what God has given to 'mankind in common'. He wrote, ' For this labour being the unquestionable

Later, Thomas Malthus[5] posited that nature is characterized by scarcity, and that unchecked population growth must produce disasters, such as disease, famine and war. The reason lay in the insufficiency of natural resources. As population grew, people would struggle for insufficient supplies of food and materials, resulting in shortage and collapse.

Both Locke and Malthus, and many others, envisaged the operation of supply and demand in catastrophic terms, and perceived control, whether enjoined by proprietary restrictions or government fiat, as necessary to society's survival. This repressive philosophy of existence is implicit in copyright law's long tradition of limitation and foreclosure, and disregard of the public's wishes. Theory, neatly enough, seemed to fall into line. Even the seemingly self-evident idea that production ceases if investment is not defended from free-riding seemed to buttress the doctrine of scarcity.

The idea that strict property rights are necessary to deter free-riding is, in reality, misleading.[6] However, until the age of the internet, this and other articles of copyright faith were not subject to practical examination. The internet, however, has swept aside many of the precepts of copyright law.

Digital communication, involving electronic reproduction on a theoretically limitless scale, radically undermined the argument that proprietary control over the supply of information protected against exhaustion or undersupply. Information in cyberspace flowed constantly, seemingly endlessly between millions of users. Day-to-day, internet users vitiated in practice the idea that P2P activity must destroy sources of legitimate supply.

Rife online piracy did not, as theory predicts, destroy production. The amount of original copyright material did not decrease while the number of copies, many illicit, increased exponentially. The free flow of information, and the proliferation of unauthorized copying, did not result in diminution of internet commerce or shrinkage of copyright industries.[7]

The access corporations, such as Google, embraced the economics of limitless information and while benefitting from the protections of copyright law discovered that it created obstacles to free supply. Counterpoised against the publishing and film industries, which attacked its activities with copyright infringement actions, Google rapidly rose to the status of commercial leviathan, in economic power and political influence at least equal to, and probably exceeding, the industries with which it found itself in conflict.[8]

---

property of the labourer, no man but he can have a right to what that is once joined to, at least where there is enough, and as good left in common for others' (Locke 1689/1988, Sec. 27).

[5] Malthus (1798/1999).

[6] See Atkinson (2007, *supra*) for examination of incentive theory of copyright.

[7] The music industry reported consistent falls in CD sales but the industry increased revenues in other areas such as concerts, merchandising and music streaming.

[8] In 2005, the Authors' Guild and American Association of Publishers launched an action against Google for breach of copyright (*Authors Guild et al v Google*, USDC). In 2004 Google announced its intention to create a global 'library to last forever' by contracting to digitize the collections of a

Acceptance of the reality of information super-abundance on the internet changed software code and, much more slowly, legal code. More importantly, recognition of super-abundance changed practices. Google did not stand for the public but public access corporations supplied to the public a more powerful way of disavowing needless and oppressive copyright restrictions—that is, restrictions based on monopoly pricing and controlled undersupply—than legislative exceptions such as fair use or fair dealing.[9]

Copyright industries began themselves to consider constructively ways to reconcile their goal of remuneration with the reality that illicit public access to material is made possible by digital technology and communication. In the digital world, encryption may exclude some of the people for some of the time, but, as a general rule, access cannot permanently be denied. Industry representatives are thus reconsidering assumptions, such as the idea that unauthorized copying is prima facie theft.

If information, communicated digitally, is limitless, legal rules said to guarantee supply may become redundant. If one supplier of copyright material wishes to control supply on restrictive terms, many others may wish to supply permissively. In this way, information markets created by use of the internet may begin to resemble a free market, or one in which transaction costs are, more often than not, negligible. Commerce, dominated by main suppliers of goods and services, dependent on proprietary rights, may become atomised. If information is limitless, control, the object of proprietary regulation, is attenuated. Industries, enforcing proprietary rights, become less powerful. The market is free because exchange is free, although its purpose is to fix a price.

number of great libraries (initially Harvard, Stanford, Michigan and Oxford university libraries and New York Public Library) and make them publicly searchable (out of print works in the public domain would be available for reading or downloading). The parties agreed in 2010 a preliminary settlement creating a compensation fund of $125 million for authors and publishers and creating a books rights registry. In 2011, the US District Court rejected the settlement and in 2013, the 2nd circuit appeals court rejected the lower court's certification of authors as a class in the action. The appeals court beginning September 2013 began heard argument about whether Google's book search program constituted fair (or as Google argued, transformative) use. In 2007, in *Viacom International Inc.* v. *YouTube Inc.*, Viacom and other film corporations sued YouTube—by then owned by Google—for US$1 billion in the New York Southern District Court. Viacom alleged YouTube is liable for secondary copyright infringement for the uploading of videos on its site by users infringing the copyright of Viacom and others. The District Court ruled in 2010 that DCMA safe harbor provisions protected You Tube summarily dismissing the Viacom action. The second circuit appeals court vacated the summary dismissal in 2012 and remanded aspects of the ruling to the first instance judge. The appeals court found that if You Tube knew of, or was wilfully blind to, uploading of infringing material, safe harbor protection would not apply. However, In 2013, the judge at first instance again found against Viacom. You Tube did not have actual knowledge of infringement and did not induce infringement. Viacom appealed.

[9] It should not be thought that access corporations like Google obey internal logic different from corporations that profit from controlling access to information. The Google Book Settlement apparently signalled Google's intent to benefit public interest in digital preservation and dissemination of the world's supply of books. Google's motivation, however, proved not less mercenary than that of copyright industries. Its copying or preservation project, as it is implemented, undoubtedly confers benefit on the world's public. On the other hand, Google made no gratuitous gift to the public, controlling, for profit, supply of books digitised.

13.3 Open Access

Since the beginning of the twenty-first century, a group of researchers across the world have embraced 'Open Access', a movement dedicated to free online distribution of journal articles. Open Access is a reaction to constriction in supply of academic information caused by rise in subscription costs.

As publishers increased online access fees, libraries subscribed to fewer digital academic works. Authors of articles, as much as readers, grew frustrated at supply restriction. Scholars, eager for more dissemination, began to make copies of their works, usually articles, available online.

Many did not ask publishers for permission to do so, believing that authorship entitled them to disseminate works for free to a global audience. Publishers did not protest until some voices suggested that open access vitiated publisher rights. In the meantime, institutions also began to support open access. Some funding bodies insisted that funds recipients must implement open access policies, and employers such as universities required academic employees to agree to grant licences to works produced. Academics and others swiftly began to consider open access in relation to material other than articles, including data and books. In some countries, government began permitting open access to various types of government information.

How material is made available for open access varies. Supporters advocate that material is uploaded accompanied by a statement that access is free, and stating copyright or other permissions. The technical format is to facilitate reuse. However, while most academics rigorously ensure that material is made available for free, only a few concern themselves with stating licensing conditions or ensuring a format permits reuse.

13.4 Creative Commons

Like the Open Access movement, Creative Commons, launched in the United States in 2002 by academics and others, has tried to solve the problem of constricting supply of copyright material. Supply constriction is caused by copyright holders—usually industries—exercising rights to practise price discrimination, limit competition, or punish infringement.

Creative Commons enables copyright holders to release copyright works to the public by affixing to those works one of six types of copyright licences available for use on the Creative Commons website.[10] All licences require attribution of authorship but they otherwise vary in type, four requiring that works must not be used for

[10] Major web platforms such as Flickr, Wikipedia and Youtube embedded CC licensing as an option in their input or upload functions. Anyone contributing to Wikipedia must license their input under a CC BY SA licence. Hundreds of millions of CC items are now available online. Any

commercial purposes. Electronic documents identifiable as Creative Commons-licensed can be used, consistent with licence requirements, permission-free, that is, without obtaining permission other than that supplied by the licence.[11]

The purpose of open licensing is to facilitate the legal dissemination of works, creating a bursting and vibrant 'commons' of information.[12] Inspired by the open-source and free software movements, the Creative Commons movement confidently predicts that liberated from rigid normative restraints, such as onerously enforced copyright law, people will share information for individual gain as well as the public good. This belief in the benefits of sharing and access is one that government, cultural institutions and many artists share. In theory a culture of open access encourages innovation although some argue that strictly enforced proprietary rights are the corollary, if not precursor, of innovation.

Although Creative Commons is concerned with the social and cultural benefits of freely sharing knowledge or information, it does not prevent the commercial exploitation of copyright material for commercial purposes, or purposes that contemplate commercial benefit. Web 2.0 entrepreneurs willingly utilize CC licences. Trent Reznor, lead singer of the band *Nine Inch Nails* released his instrumental album Ghosts I–IV under CC licence—nine songs without a fee and 18 songs with a small fee—and was able to recoup millions of dollars in the sales through his website of associated products and services. His success gives an indication of how copyright law of the future might look—a permissive copyright law—and what its function might be.

Enthusiastic public reaction to Open Access and Creative Commons licensing shows popular desire to share knowledge and culture in the online world. In particular, Creative Commons, which starts with the legally valid premise that access to information is a human right, shows how legal restrictions on information flow may legally be circumvented.

In other words, it works with, and not against, copyright law to produce results that most can accept. It does not resolve philosophical differences over the extent to which property rights should regulate the information economy. But it does offer a middle way that allow people and institutions to steer a productive course between copyright advocate and abolitionists. The success of Creative Commons also suggests the possibility of a future, permissive, copyright law that encourages sharing and dissemination of information for private and public purposes.

---

advanced search engine function can now be set to find CC licenced images, songs, videos, articles and other copyright material.

[11] The Creative Commons licence designations, identifiable as distinctive icons on the face of an electronic document, or embedded in document metadata, are machine-readable. Creative Commons' licences are: Attribution (CC BY), Attribution Share Alike (CC BY-SA, Attribution No Derivatives (CC BY-ND), Attribution Non-Commercial (CC BY-NC), Attribution Non-Commercial Share Alike (CC BY-NC-SA), Attribution Non-Commercial No Derivatives (CC BY-NC-ND).

[12] Creative Commons draws inspiration from the idea that in the absence of property enclosures, historically the annexation of common lands for profit, society creates (or recreates) commons, of land or information, that are shared by all, and free for all.

13.5 Social Networking

One criticism that could be made of copyright regulation since its inception is that its effect is anti-social. The producer exercises monopoly rights to determine price and supply. Public preferences are important, but not necessarily determinative. Limits on copying and distribution stymie types of free social exchange, including adaptation of works.

Conversely, copyright advocates argue that monopoly control for specified periods is necessary to create efficient information markets. Monopoly secures continued production, and its absence results in free-riding (piracy), and destruction of productive incentive. Monopoly control over production results in profit, investment and continued production. Copyright regulation thus maximises public welfare.[13]

Whether or not the incentive argument is accepted, it can hardly be ignored that, to the extent that copyright law creates an impersonal nexus between production and consumption, it undermines communal experience of, and contribution to, culture. In cultures dependent on community participation social alienation is less common.

In the digital world, consumers of copyright material are no longer estranged. Online communication occupies untold millions in social networking, that is, exchanging information by digital network, for the most part via the internet but also by networks connecting mobile devices such as smartphones and tablets. Digital social networking seems to have arisen, as if inevitably, to fulfil social impulses.

13.6 Facebook

Social networking occurs in many forms but is synonymous with the internet social networking site, Facebook. Facebook is a 'platform' created and launched in 2004 by Harvard student Mark Zuckerberg, with collaboration and investment of others. Facebook in 2012 reported over one billion subscribers or users,[14] suggesting a possibility—and even likelihood—that within decades, most of the world's population will use digital networks to engage in varied forms of communication.

[13] The argument for monopoly control is, to a certain extent, normative, since governments rely on it to justify regulation. Importantly, the incentive argument, allowing for its implicit assumptions, does not take account of the social or communicative nature of copyright-protected material, and the desire of most people to copy, distribute and share that material.

[14] *Digital Market Ramblings* reported in 2013 a Facebook monthly user figure of 1.11 billion.

The site facilitates a mode of continuous interaction, textual, graphic, audiovisual, that allows individuals to satisfy a human appetite for social exchange, performance and assertion.[15]

So far as copyright regulation is concerned, Facebook, although structured using open source software, and offering users freedom to add textual and audiovisual material to their pages, prohibits use of copyright infringing material on user pages and reserves (and exercises) power to remove prohibited pages. While in theory, its invitation to upload varieties of information contemplates copyright mayhem, Facebook allies itself to a corporate ethos that invariably upholds proprietary rights.

Even so, Facebook's success suggests how modes of digital communication, even if intended to conform to copyright law, may undermine that law. As noted, copyright law, to the extent that it restricts or prohibits information flow, that is, adopts a non-permissive attitude to dissemination, is anti-social.

Social networking entities such as Facebook, which show themselves willing to enforce copyright prohibitions, cannot escape tension between focus on compliance and control, and user demands for permissive attitudes towards information exchange. More importantly, the character of network communication, or radial transmission of information, is social and permissive, even if the network is closed. In principle, networking undermines copyright.[16]

References

Atkinson B (2007) The true history of copyright: the Australian experience 1905–2005. Sydney University Press, Sydney

Locke J (1689/1988) Two treatises of government. Cambridge University Press, Cambridge

Malthus T (1798/1999) In: Geoffrey G (ed) An essay on the principle of population. Oxford University Press, Oxford

[15] While Facebook is said to be a social networking site, its extraordinary popularity perhaps derives from the opportunity it provides for self to speak publicly. On Facebook, actor overshadows interaction. In a psychological sense, the site supplies means for self-exposition and self-exploration, and channels of narcissistic supply.

[16] Twitter, like Facebook a source of ceaseless, publicly available (and contingently available) online discourse, illustrates the proposition that proprietary interactive platforms, while observant of copyright prescriptions, obey an expository logic inconsistent with copyright's logic of exclusivity. They create in many users a tendency to resist restriction, and view expressive freedom as something akin to a human right. Twitter allows users, via website or external devices, to tweet messages of not more than 140 characters to followers. Tweets have created a new form of public discourse, commentary that is abbreviated, sometimes epigrammatic, and, by turns, frivolous, trivial, informative or consequential.

Chapter 14
The Meaning and Future of Copyright

14.1 Aaron Swartz

In the past three decades, since the ascendancy of the United States in the process of determining international copyright policy and rules, considerable bitterness has entered debate about copyright. Many individuals have objected to the attitude of the United States government to copyright legal infraction around the world. Many Americans have also protested at their government's vehement attitude to real or alleged copyright infringements of US citizens.

Anger swelled at the government's prosecution (2011–2013) of Aaron Swartz. Aaron Swartz was a programmer of prodigious ability, 'a kid genius',[1] and later advocate for public freedom from corporate or government oppression.[2] On 11 January 2013, he hanged himself in his Brooklyn apartment, aged 26.

Between September 2010 and January 2011, Swartz logged into the Massachussets Institute of Technology's digital network to download millions of public domain academic articles from the JSTOR digital library. He connected remotely and by direct wire link. Download volumes exceeded guest user privileges and conventional download limits. In early January 2011, MIT recorded him entering and leaving a network wiring closet where he attached concealed a laptop for download. Notified by MIT, police arrested him.

Once Swartz supplied to JSTOR the hard drive cache of files downloaded, JSTOR declared itself uninterested in pursuing legal action against him. The US Attorney for Massachusetts, however, prosecuted under computer and wire fraud legislation. A 2011 Massachusetts Grand Jury indictment alleged six violations, increased in 2012 by nine felony counts.

---

[1] Lessig blog 12 January 2013, http://lessig.tumblr.com.

[2] Swartz became involved, aged 15, in the coding of Creative Commons. He was later known as a contributor to development of RSS and Reddit software. He advocated for open access in the Guerilla Open Access Manual (2008) and in 2010 he helped to found Demand Progress, an internet advocacy organisation dedicated to 'win[ning] progressive policy changes for ordinary people ... '.

B. Atkinson and B. Fitzgerald, *A Short History of Copyright*,
DOI 10.1007/978-3-319-02075-4_14,

After issuing of the first indictment, the US Attorney said in a press release that Swartz, 'faces up to 35 years in prison . . . restitution, forfeiture and fine of up to $1 million.' Before his death, her office offered Swartz a plea bargain of conviction and 6 months in a low security prison.

The tragic circumstances of his death did not obscure recognition of Swartz's talents and public contributions, and he swiftly became fixed in public memory as a quintessential figure, young, bold, expressing in his life his ideals about freedom, universality and the liberating use of technology. Among members of bisecting circles of people concerned by restriction of information access and political freedom, his death caused palpable public grief and anger. Some blamed the Justice Department for precipitating suicide by pursuing pre-trial tactics of intimidation and aggression.

Debate over the Justice Department's conduct[3] essayed the proposition that many or most prosecutors try to secure plea bargains by suggesting the likelihood of lengthy sentences for a convicted felon. By implication, the Justice Department acted towards Swartz as it does to most individuals accused of crimes. Even allowing a neutral attitude on the part of prosecutors, two questions linger: why was Swartz indicted for criminal offences, and what does his treatment suggest about broader government attitudes to future information regulation?

Prosecutors charged Swartz, under the wires and computer fraud legislation, for engaging (in substance) in fraudulent property appropriation. Conceptually, the authors of Swartz's indictment document hardly distinguish between abstract and tangible property. What matters above all is the crime of theft. The indictment states twice that Swartz acted to 'steal' from JSTOR. 'Property' is defined twice, once as 'real or personal' and a second time as JSTOR's collected articles. Choice of legislation to frame charges precluded consideration of the differing policies informing legal treatment of non-excludable and excludable property. Such consideration, had it occurred, must have led to focus on harm caused, and invited consideration of intent.

The focus on theft, or 'stealing' lies at the heart of bemusement at prosecutors' attitude to Swartz. Swartz, apparently, intended a gesture against enclosure of knowledge, even if the putative encloser is a not-for-profit disseminator like JSTOR. He presumably knew that his gesture would not be regarded as morally neutral. A person seeking to download material in a way that contravenes download conditions is aware of transgression: the omission (which may be a wrong) lies in acting without consent. Such a person, however, does not perceive correlation between unauthorised downloading and, for example, hijacking a cash transport van to steal its contents.

The peculiarity in prosecutors' analysis is that they seemed unable to distinguish between an act directed towards public welfare—Swartz's mammoth downloading

[3] A considerable number of Swartz's friends, including Cory Doctorow and Lawrence Lessig blogged and spoke about the Justice Department's actions. For a partial defence of the Justice Department's actions, pointing out that the Attorney and her officers acted consistent with usual departmental prosecutorial practice, see Orin Kerr in Volokh.com 16 January 2013. James Boyle replied to Kerr in http://Huffingtonpost.com 18 January 2013.

for purpose of public dissemination—and any other act directed towards, or involving, public harm, such as hijacking a cash transport van.

To characterise Aaron Swartz, who intended public benefit, as felonious, to contemplate that his behaviour placed him in a cohort of people who might be bent against public good, is to repudiate an idea of public welfare with which he concerned himself in life. To call Swartz's downloading theft, punishable by decades of servitude, is to merge ideas about the material and transcendental. Investing academic articles, or any other kind of property, with sacerdotal value, and by extension, treating theft as sacrilege, is to distort reality.

Psychologically, Swartz's arraignment betrayed a sovereign's hatred at denial of its sovereignty. This supposition is illustrated by a blog entry in which Swartz unknowingly foretold his own unravelling in the teeth of sovereign power. After his indictment, a trial lawyer Max Kennerly suggested that Swartz read Franz Kafka's *The Trial*. A few months later, Swartz blogged about the book, 'I read it and found that it was precisely accurate – every single detail perfectly mirrored my own experience.'[4]

The Trial is a story about Josef K, who, arrested on his 30th birthday, for a year experiences waking life as if sojourning in the shadowlands of nightmare. Nothing makes sense. Nothing is explained. Power is unanswerable. The nightmare is inescapable. After fruitlessly trying to discover the reason for his arrest, K submits, on his 31st birthday, to execution.

In another play, Kafka's protagonist is condemned by his father with the words, 'I sentence you to death by drowning.' In Kafka's *Letter To His Father* (1919), he describes his father as despot, overshadowing his life. In *The Trial*, Kafka makes clear that K is murdered by inimical exercise of power that issues from a single source of authority—its own will. Kafka's father displays the same monstrous will. He does not propose his son's execution, but Kafka does not doubt that resistance to his will is a capital offence.

Parallels between the situation of Aaron Swartz and the literature of Kafka need not be laboured. At the same time, the death of Swartz, and his treatment by the Justice Department, crystallise years of debate over the content and meaning of copyright policy and law. Aaron Swartz's downloads from JSTOR were intended to demonstrate the moral foolishness of refusing to share information. He acted boldly and found himself dragged, by authority of the United States, into a world of Kafka's devising.

His own country did not say, 'I sentence you to death by drowning.' Inimical power, exercised by the Justice Department, promised, in effect, to punish him for life. At the end of Swartz's review of *The Trial*, he observed, 'K . . . decides to stop fighting the system and just live his life without asking for permission. It goes well . . . for a while.'

---

[4] See *Litigation and Trial* blog of Max Kennerly, 14 January 2011, and the 2011 Review of Books at http://www.aaronsw.com.

If legal rules are permissive, in the sense that they permit humans to express the dignity of their natures, a 'life without asking for permission' is possible. Such a life is what Aaron Swartz appears to have wanted for everyone. The copyright system, as it has evolved to the present, appears to make difficult for its adherents thought of a world 'without asking for permission.'

14.2 Purpose

A decade of P2P cases, in which defendants consisted of music and film downloaders, producers of software that facilitated illegal downloading and ISPs that connected subscribers to the internet, shed little light on the question that occurred to internet users delighted by the seemingly miraculous utility of the internet: what is the purpose of copyright?

For more than 40 years preceding the end of the first decade of the twenty-first century, scholars examined the philosophy and economics of copyright, reaching conclusions mostly at odds with the premises adopted by government and judiciary. Non-legal analysis rarely accepted uncritically the favoured assertions of copyright apologists, that copyrights encourage production and dissemination, and the law balances the interests of producer and consumer. As a number of observers noted, these assertions were hypotheses, unvalidated by empirical evidence.

The courts in the P2P decade refrained from examining the question of purpose deeply and ignored derivative questions: *Why* is unauthorized downloading illegal? *Why* are copyright proprietors entitled to proscribe unauthorized copying that occurs outside a legally definable market? *Do* copyrights confer a right of automatic remuneration or a merely a right to negotiate for reward? *Has* any legislature or court ever settled these and other questions?

Arguments in P2P cases mostly followed conventional lines, complainants alleging harm caused by invasion of proprietary rights and defendants raising the defence of fair use (in the case of direct infringers) or innocent facilitation. Argument did not depart from interpretation of the scope and application of established doctrines, such as fair use, and adjudication, not surprisingly, focused on legal principle, not philosophical or theoretical exegesis.

Yet copyright law in the age of the internet could, from the perspective of internet users, hardly advance meaningfully unless legislature and courts could emancipate themselves from the restrictions of precedent-based legal reasoning. Digital technology called into question the presumptions of copyright law, and internet users, who rejected the validity of laws that constrained access, dissemination and use, increasingly rejected the pecuniary demands of proprietary interests and restrictions on supply of information (see Barlow 1994).

Those users expressed a public voice, a public volition, until now unheard and ignored by government or private interests. In a sense, the internet made copyright politics 'interactive', for whatever the law said, or politicians or corporations assumed, the diffuse public of internet users—including by necessity, inventive programmers—showed itself capable of flouting laws and doctrine, and finding new ways of securing access to information. Other users, such as writers of 'fan fiction'—a new genre involving creative segues from the published works—present another challenge to precepts of copyright law, one that courts may not welcome.[5]

The rise of public access corporations confirmed the trend towards public insistence upon the individual right to what might be called freedom of information—or weightless information. As companies such as Google demonstrated, information is super-abundant, and consumers of information endlessly curious and inventive in its uses. The internet is destroying the old idea, which animated the copyright law for 300 years, that information is a scarce commodity to be protected with more and more extensive rights. This old idea persists in government thinking, in the discourse of copyright industries and in social precepts. Its disappearance is by no means inevitable so long as proprietary attitudes hostile to public access and freedoms—in short, the attitude of privatization—dominate society at large.

On the other hand, unless humankind discovers the means of deconstituting individuals and reconstituting them near-instantaneously in a new location—as depicted in science fiction fantasies such as *Star Trek*—it is difficult to imagine invention of a more extraordinary mode of communication than digital storage and transmission. This means that the literal wonders of digital communication must invite more and more public participation and create burgeoning counterweight to the privatization impulse. This struggle between public and private will determine the future shape of copyright law and, ultimately, perhaps its existence.

14.3 Conclusion

That copyright law might cease to regulate information dissemination seems unlikely. The history of property relations is one of extending control over whatever is controllable. To some, last century's collectivist interregnum foretold abolition of

[5] Although a case involving what could probably be better characterized as an example of derivative fiction, rather than fan fiction, *Salinger v. Colting,* 2010 WL 1729126, 9 (2d Cir. April 30, 2010) demonstrates judicial reluctance to permit creative appropriation of fictional characters and their back-stories. In *Salinger*, the Second Circuit Court of Appeals returned a copyright infringement case to the New York District Court to reconsider its finding of 'irreparable harm' (on which basis the district court granted an injunction against publication of a 'sequel' to the J.D. Salinger novel *Catcher in the Rye*). The District Court found that the defendant, Frederick Colting, author of *60 Years Later: Coming Through the Rye*, breached copyright in J.D. Salinger's novel *The Catcher in the Rye*—and, more controversially, copyright in the character of Holden Caulfield, the protagonist of Salinger's work. *60 Years Later* imagined Caulfield as a man aged 76 ('Mr C'), escaped from his nursing home and wandering the streets of New York. In Salinger's novel, Caulfield is a 17 year old, expelled from school and wandering in New York. The District Court rejected arguments of fair use for the purpose of commentary and criticism (or parody). Though it vacated the lower court's decision, the appeals court found *60 Years Later* to be substantially similar to Salinger's novel. The Salinger trust was 'likely to succeed on the merits of his copyright infringement claim'. On fan fiction, and user-generated content, see Wong (2009), p. 1075.

property and emancipation from exactions of power and wealth. However, gulag, famine and murder extinguished belief in a society in which nothing is owned. In the twenty-first century, the regime of private property seems irreducible and illimitable, furnishing means to control the universe itself, should technology allow.

Why this should be so is nothing less than the story of politics, or the contest for sovereignty. Sovereignty is more than power to command. It is also power to possess and exclude, the constituents of ownership. Contest for sovereignty resulted almost invariably—until adoption, in the last 200 or more years, of the principle of equality—in shades of absolutism. Until some modern societies created a sovereignty of many, allocating rights of equality to their members, struggle for sovereign power ended in rule by tyrant or coterie.[6]

Copyright law created another tyranny, that of eternal market sovereignty. Copyright's span is finite. Yet monopolies that outlive populations may as well be called eternal. Since the time of the Stationers' monopoly, advocates repeated one article of belief: creative effort conjures varied and delightful fruit, which is easily plucked without licence, unless forever protected from pilfering. The copyright sovereign demands eternal sovereignty.

Belief in immutability is characteristic of sovereign power throughout history. Yet even everlasting sovereignties disappear. Some tyrannies may end suddenly, as if expunged by outraged nature. Others vanish slowly, and in part, like Roman monocracy, its traces imprinted in emerging patterns of feudalism. Always, contradiction becomes too much. Gross poverty contradicts gross wealth. Weakness contradicts power. Paraphrasing Marx, sovereignties produce their own gravediggers.[7]

Copyright's gravediggers, say its opponents, are millions of users of digital technology who circumvent, dissent, copy, upload, download, share, flout and jeer. A more accurate statement may be that if law reserves for the sovereign too much power, that sovereign, in this case the copyright system, is like a despot, and the day comes when the despot, refusing to share power, is hunted to terminus, a grave dug by those it declared lawless.

Problems arising from power concentration are not resolved without sharing. Sharing sovereignty, by grant of suffrage and other rights, erases its inimical character. No sovereign shares willingly. On the other hand, nothing commends a

---

[6] In antiquity, political struggle created near universal tyranny, except in Athens and Rome. Citizens of the former city invented plebiscite democracy, permitting a small group of qualified men a right to vote. After a few decades, democracy of the few collapsed into tyranny. In Rome, aristocrats and people shared republican government for centuries, before aristocratic assertion of sovereignty resulted in ruinous civil wars, and finally tyranny of emperors. Feudalism established, in most of the world, control arrangements, conferring on small groups, emperors, kings and lords, control over land and labour. Until partial acceptance of the idea of popular sovereignty, all political systems assumed overlordship of one or a few. Even today, the vesting pattern of property rights suggests that popular sovereignty is unrealised. In all countries, ownership is highly concentrated.

[7] Marx and Engels (1848), Chapter 1.

tyrant's recalcitrance. A fixed policy of proscription is usually fatal to the proscriber. The Bourbons proscribed and were proscribed. 'They had,' said Talleyrand, expert in accommodation, 'learned nothing, and forgotten nothing.'[8]

Comparison between Bourbons and copyright industries is faint speculation. A more concrete observation is that human freedom, object of the great formative constitutional documents of the United States and France, could become a motif for reform that helps copyright regulation to last. Copyright restricts human freedom to the extent that its prohibitions and punishments, and scope of rights, contradict ordinary expectation of what is legitimate.

In short, if copyright regulation is adapted to offer users freedom, akin to expressive political freedoms guaranteed in rights of free speech, communication and access to information, it may yet endure by consent. Consent may grow, if regulators continue to discuss, for reform purposes, the length of copyright monopoly. Regulation that reduced the central role of permission and control could not fail to win admiration in some quarters.

In 130 years since the Berne Convention, those who determine copyright policy and laws have shown small inclination to reduce scope of laws, once made. Regulation and deregulation alike begin as acts of executive will. The executive, however, proposes laws more prolifically than it seeks their repeal. The young will grow old before they see the light of Halley's Comet, or rejection of copyright precepts.

Thus legal code will enjoin, as before, preservation of sovereignty, not its diffusion. Identifying unlawful actions of tens or hundreds of millions of network users may be thought unfeasible. Crowds camouflage illegal acts. In reality, copyright prohibitions are more enforceable than many realise. Few hackers escape legal consequences if the executive—or industries—will their identification.

Those who argue that code will be used to preclude freedoms hitherto available to internet or software users emphasise the power of software writers to disable communications technology. According to internet pessimists, the possibilities offered by network communication will reduce as networks become restricted or controlled by surveillance gateways. Governments, may, for approved security purposes spy on private online activity. User records of network owners or managers may, with growing licence, be interrogated by security agencies, or inquirers investigating copyright infringement. Digital rights management software will circumscribe multifarious use. Laws will prohibit most unremunerated use.

This stygian future is possible if governments, industries, or other actors determined to control information supply, enlarge their sovereignty over supply. Such a future is perhaps growing unlikely, however, for two reasons. The first is that, as the rise of access corporations show, if digital technology creates means for

[8] Observation attributed to Charles Maurice de Talleyrand-Périgord, Minister of Foreign Affairs and Prime Minister of France. It is possible Talleyrand is not author of the saying. He is supposed to have made the statement after accession of Charles X, the last Bourbon, in 1824, or his deposition in 1830.

inexhaustible information supply, supply finds demand. The second is that digital technology is agent of metamorphosis and new creation: in the internet's insterstices, injunctions of law or programming vanish.

If code is interdiction, it fails. The ganglions of digital creation are too numerous to be uprooted. As well forbid growth of sunflowers and dandelions, bursting in hues of yellow and gold. The argument that code is increasingly restrictive depends on the premise that statutory prohibitions are enforceable and software exclusions effective. Code has power to preclude digital uses. This premise is demonstrably correct, but only in part. Copyright laws are enforced to preclude piracy or unauthorised copying. Software programs prevent use of, or access to, digital material, unless the user complies with contractual terms specified by the supplier.

In due course, however, non-preclusion, dream and nightmare of science fiction may become reality. Non-preclusion means that code cannot preclude. Code is deprived of power to proscribe use or forestall decryption. In theory, software might develop autonomic generative function, that is, autonomous function, outside human control, responsive to voice command, anticipating human wishes, generating its own behaviour, and implementing its own repairs, modifications or improvements.

Autonomic generativity would create individual crypto-life-forms, subservient to human beings, and outside the jurisdiction of regulatory systems intended to govern human behaviour. Science fiction conceptions of machinery developing volition and personhood also posits that autonomic machines or systems must eventually face moral choices. More starkly, they must choose to do good or evil.

A more modest conception debars rational possibility of volition and moral choice, and asserts that while autonomic function is likely to place software systems outside jurisdiction, nothing prevents voluntary code replacing enforceable code, or co-operation substituting effectively for code-protected monopolies and exclusions.

At the very least, a future in which software code is, in function, permissive not restrictive, will more likely pertain than one in which a technology facilitating communicative emancipation is co-opted to limit expressive freedom. Global users of digital technology express support for the principle of non-preclusion by showing preference for what might be called permissive technology, specifically, communication devices that enable more untrammelled communication and use. Users may as well be revolutionaries rattling palace gates.

References

Barlow JP (1994) The economy of ideas: a framework for patents and copyrights in the digital age (everything you know about intellectual property is wrong). WIRED, 2.03, pp 1–13

Marx K, Engels F (1848) The communist manifesto. London

Wong M (2009) Transformative user generated content in copyright law: infringing derivative works or fair use? Vanderbilt J Entertain Technol Law 11(4):1075–1139

Chapter 15
Conclusion

This book tells the story of how, over centuries, people, society and culture created laws affecting supply of information. In the twenty-first century, uniform global copyright laws are claimed to be indispensable to the success of entertainment, internet and other information industries. Do copyright laws encourage information flow? Many say that copyright laws limit dissemination, harming society. In the last 300 years, industries armed with copyrights controlled output and distribution. Now the internet's disruption of economic patterns may radically reshape information regulation. Information freedom, a source of emancipation, may change the world.

B. Atkinson and B. Fitzgerald, *A Short History of Copyright*,
DOI 10.1007/978-3-319-02075-4_15,

Index

B. Atkinson and B. Fitzgerald, *A Short History of Copyright*,
DOI 10.1007/978-3-319-02075-4, © Springer International Publishing Switzerland 2014

The manufacturer's authorised representative in the EU is Springer Nature Customer Service Centre GmbH, Europaplatz 3, 69115 Heidelberg, Germany. If you have any concerns regarding our products, please contact ProductSafety@springernature.com

Printed and bound by CPI Group (UK) Ltd, Croydon, CR0 4YY
30/09/2026
02225468-0018